Northern Olympic Peninsula

An Explorer's Guide

Mike & Kristy Westby

Copyright © 2021 Mike & Kristy Westby

All rights reserved.

No part of this publication may be reproduced, distributed, linked to or transmitted in any form or by any means, including photocopying, recording or other electronic or mechanical methods, without the prior written permission of the author and/or publisher, except for brief quotations embodied in critical reviews and certain noncommercial uses permitted by copyright law.

No part of this publication may be made available for downloading online without the permission of Mike & Kristy Westby.

Although every precaution has been taken to verify the accuracy of the information contained herein, no responsibility is assumed for any errors or omissions, and no liability is assumed for damages that may result from the use of this information.

Discover the Olympic Peninsula by Day –
Stay in Historic Hotels by Night™

The majority of the photos within
this book are copyright Mike & Kristy Westby

ISBN-13: 978-1733598392

060121 - CS

Cover graphics by Sarah Craig – SarahCookDesign.com

"Twenty years from now, you will be more disappointed by the things you didn't do than those you did. So throw off the bowlines. Sail away from the safe harbor. Catch the trade winds in your sails. Explore. Dream. Discover.

Mark Twain

Northern Olympic Peninsula
– An Explorer's Guide

Lake Crescent - Olympic National Park

The Olympic Peninsula is a land of diverse landscapes, each showcasing a world of incomparable majesty, rugged grandeur and graceful beauty. Ocean waves from the mighty Pacific crash against sea stacks before breaking upon rocky shores, graceful yet powerful orcas, humpbacks and gray whales ply the deep waters of the Salish Sea, and the snow covered peaks of the Olympic Mountains tower over verdant green valleys home to lush forests and cascading waterfalls.

With *so many* destinations and attractions, how do you begin to discover what to see, do and explore first ? The answer...the **Northern Olympic Peninsula - An Explorer's Guide**. We've listed over 150 fun, exciting and fascinating attractions, destinations, and sites for you to visit, complete with descriptions, contact information, tips and usually a photo or two. Visit Olympic National Park, explore historic lighthouses, tour a vintage airplane museum, kayak on the Salish Sea, stand in the quietest place in the United States, watch how wooden boats are made, see orcas, gray whales, and humpbacks up close, sleep in your very own castle, discover dramatic beaches and coves, and enjoy amazing panoramic vistas.

Enjoy exploring the Northern Olympic Peninsula!

www.Discover-Washington.com

Map Courtesy of InsideOut Solutions

CONTENTS

Destinations

Port Gamble & Port Townsend	26
Fort Worden at Port Townsend	64
Sequim	76
Port Angeles	98
Lake Crescent, Sol Duc, & Olympic National Park	108
Elwha River, Joyce, Clallam Bay, & Sekiu	120
Neah Bay, Cape Flattery, & Shi Shi Beach	132
Lake Ozette, Rialto Beach, Forks, & The Hoh Rainforest	140

Additional Information

Olympic Peninsula Permits & Passes	15
Taking the Ferry	18
Helpful Phone Numbers	162

How to Use This Guide

You may use this guide in two different ways...

Choose Your Northern Olympic Peninsula Destination - Pick a destination, such as Port Townsend, Sequim, Neah Bay, Lake Crescent, or the Hoh Rainforest, and then open this book to discover all of the sites you can visit at your destination for the day, weekend, or longer.

Or

Choose Your Northern Olympic Peninsula Activity - Flip through the pages of the *Northern Olympic Peninsula - An Explorer's Guide*, choose which activities you'd like to experience, and then venture forth! Want to see the most beautiful waterfall on the peninsula? Then head to Olympic National Park and visit Sol Duc Falls. Want to see a pod of orcas dramatically plying the waters of the Salish Sea? Then book a whale watching trip out of Port Townsend or Port Angeles. Maybe you'd like to stand in the quietest place in the United States? If so, then make your way to a very specific spot in the Hoh Rain Forest. Or maybe you want to walk a long and beautiful sandy beach as the ocean waves crash nearby. If that's the case, then you'll want to discover remote Shi Shi Beach. Find what excites your adventurous spirit and explore the Northern Olympic Peninsula!

It's an Attractions Guide

While there are hundreds of hikes on the Olympic Peninsula, this book is not a hiking guide, (though we do include some classics!) but instead reveals over 150 interesting attractions, sites and destinations on the northern Olympic Peninsula. Inside these pages you'll discover and explore the busy Victorian seaport of Port Townsend, visit a historic lighthouse, tour a vintage airplane museum, kayak on the Strait of Juan de Fuca, see majestic orcas, humpbacks, and gray whales, sleep in your very own castle, stand in the quietest place in the United States, ride in a hot air balloon, explore unique shops, eat at great restaurants, meet friendly people, and so much more!

Timing

A visit to the northern Olympic Peninsula is a beautiful trip most anytime of the year, with the conditions changing noticeably from season to season. Spring, summer and early fall can bring beautiful sunny days, while winter's cooler temperatures are often moderated by the waters of the strait of Juan de Fuca. Expect plenty of clouds and rainfall during the fall and winter months in the Olympic Mountains and all points west, (They don't call it a rainforest for nothing!) while areas to the east remain somewhat drier due to the natural "rain shadow" created by the Olympics. Be sure to check the weather forecast before setting out on your day of exploration.

www.Discover-Washington.com

BRING YOUR BINOCULARS

From dramatic ocean vistas and distant alpine peaks to soaring majestic eagles and spouting gray whales, there is much to see when exploring the beautiful Olympic Peninsula, so you may want to consider bringing a good pair of binoculars with you when you set out for the day.

WHALE WATCHING

Photo courtesy of Puget Sound Express / Renee Beitzel

The northern Olympic Peninsula is rich in opportunities to spot whales as you make your way along the "Whale Trail". Humpbacks, grays, minkes and of course orcas all ply the waters of the Pacific Ocean, Strait of Juan de Fuca, and Puget Sound. Be sure to pack your binoculars, and learn more at www.TheWhaleTrail.org

www.Discover-Washington.com

Gray Whales

Every year, an estimated 22,000 gray whales migrate up and down the Washington coast year-round as they make their way from Canada to Mexico and back, with most being spotted from mid-December through January, from late March to June, and then through the summer months, with September being a high point of the year. In addition, some gray whales make the Strait of Juan de Fuca their home year-round. As a result, keep an eye out for gray whales anytime you are in sight of salt water.

Humpback Whales

The "Humpback Comeback" is in full swing in the Strait of Juan de Fuca! Whereas years ago you would never see one of these magnificent animals in the area, today there are hundreds, most of which can be spotted near the east end of the strait during the summer and fall months of June through November.

Minke Whales

While common throughout the world, the minke whale isn't spotted here very often, so if you see one, it is a real treat. Keep an eye out for them in the waters near Port Angeles.

Orcas

Not a whale, but instead a cousin of the bottle-nosed dolphin, orcas are often spotted within Puget Sound, the San Juan Islands, and the east end of the Strait of Juan de Fuca. With their striking black and white coloring and distinctive dorsal fins, these highly intelligent, social and sometimes playful animals are one of the treasured icons of the Pacific Northwest.

www.Discover-Washington.com

Take Your Time and Enjoy The Sights

As you make your way through this guidebook, you'll see a small clock icon placed next to some of the listings. There are many northern Olympic Peninsula attractions that do not require much time to visit. A stop at Madison Creek Falls by the Elwha River may require about half an hour, while a visit to the Historical Fire Bell Tower in Port Townsend may require half that, but locations and adventures such as Cape Flattery, Dungeness Spit and whale watching in the Strait of Juan de Fuca absolutely call for you to spend more time enjoying these commanding views or once-in-a-lifetime experiences. Wherever you see the clock icon within these pages, plan on spending at least an hour at that location, and we would encourage you to spend even more time there while enjoying the scenery, walking the beach or even kayaking while looking for orcas. If it means missing out on some of the other places on your list, then so be it. They'll be waiting for you on your visit to the Olympic Peninsula!

Public and Private Beaches

Unlike the state of Oregon to the south, some of the beaches on the Olympic Peninsula are privately owned and, as a result, are not open to the public, so please be mindful of any signs indicating a private beach with restricted access. That said, many beaches, including any within the Olympic National Park, the Olympic National Forest, any Washington State Park, a public campground, etc. are open to the public.

CONSIDER SOME GOOD PAPER MAPS

We can't emphasize this enough. You will want to travel with and use a couple of good paper maps, and the more detailed, the better. Your phone will no doubt work well, but you may be exploring some remote parts of the northern Olympic Peninsula, many of which have no cell signal whatsoever, so your phone will not work there. In addition, your paper maps will always boot up and never run out of power.

As you make your way along and stop at various locations, you'll often see folded local or Olympic Peninsula maps made available for free or for sale, especially in local Visitor Centers. These are very helpful, so grab more than one and keep them with you at all times. For more detail on the roads you'll be traveling, we also recommend the large Washington atlases put out by DeLorme. You can find them online for about $25.

Multiple official Washington tourism divisions online, including ExperienceWA.com and OlympicPeninsula.org, offer very helpful maps, magazines and trip guides. We highly recommend you visit their web sites to order some of these free guides before setting out on your trip. If you are a member of AAA, check their resources, as well. By the way, make sure your membership is up-to-date.

www.Discover-Washington.com

Olympic Peninsula Parking Permits & Passes

A number of different parking permits are required to park at different locations throughout the northern Olympic Peninsula. Unfortunately, there is not one permit that covers all areas.

Washington State Parks – Washington Parks Discovery Pass

If you plan to visit Fort Worden or any State Parks during your exploration of the peninsula, then you will need a Washington Parks Discovery Pass. This permit is honored at over 100 Washington State Parks and recreation sites that charge a parking fee. Permits are available at self-service kiosks, licensed vendors, or offices located at the site in which a permit is required. In addition, they may be purchased by calling 866-320-9933 or online at https://www.discoverpass.wa.gov. Note that if you purchase a *daily* parking permit at one site in Washington, you may use that permit at any other site in Washington that requires the same permit *for the remainder of that day*. You do not need to buy a new permit at each site. Note, as well, that if you are staying overnight in a Fort Worden destination, your parking pass doubles as a Discovery Pass during your stay.

Online: https://www.discoverpass.wa.gov

- 1-Day Permit: $11.50
- Annual Permit: $35.00

At the Site:

- 1-Day Permit: $10.00 Cash
- Annual Permit: $30.00
  - Via credit card if a payment kiosk is available

Olympic National Park Pass

In order to visit Olympic National Park and/or Hurricane Ridge, as well as hike trails within the national park, (versus just the national forest) you will need to purchase a $30 Olympic National Park Pass. These passes admit one vehicle and all of its occupants, and *may be used at any park entrance for a period of 7 consecutive days.* Passes may be purchased at Olympic National Park visitor centers and entrance stations. Note that there is a small entrance station for Hurricane Ridge located approximately 5.5 miles up the entrance road from Port Angeles.

Your Olympic National Park Pass is valid for seven consecutive days, so be sure to keep your receipt, as it may be used elsewhere when visiting Olympic National Park.

Additional passes are required for camping and backpacking overnight within Olympic National Park.

Makah Tribe Recreational Use Permit

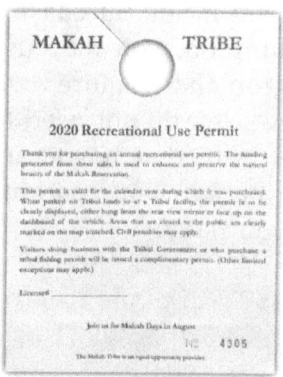

In order to park at, visit or access public recreation sites within the Makah Reservation on the northwest portion of the Olympic Peninsula, such as Cape Flattery, Shi Shi Beach, Hobuck Beach, and others, all visitors must purchase and display within their vehicle a Makah Tribe Recreational Use Permit. These annual permits may be purchased for $10 at a number of locations in Neah Bay and elsewhere, including Washburn's General Store, Makah Mini Mart, Makah Marina, and the Hobuck Beach Resort. You'll also find the Makah Cultural & Research Center Museum in Neah Bay to be a convenient location at which to purchase a permit.

Northwest Forest Pass

Of the many trailheads found within the Olympic National Forest, 16 require you to purchase and display a daily or annual Northwest Forest Pass. These may be purchased at numerous outdoor retailers, such as REI, various ranger stations on the peninsula or online. To learn which trailheads require a pass or to purchase a pass online, please visit:

www.fs.usda.gov/main/olympic/passes-permits/recreation

Note that trailheads within the Olympic National Park are covered by your Olympic National Park Pass.

Additional Passes & Entrance Fees

Note that some destinations on the peninsula, such as the Dungeness National Wildlife Refuge, require a parking fee or entrance pass specific to that site, which may or may not be covered by any of your existing passes. Credit cards are not accepted at these sites, and exact change is required. As a result, you'll find it convenient to carry some single dollar bills as you travel, as rates typically run about $3.00.

www.Discover-Washington.com

Taking a Ferry To The Northern Olympic Peninsula

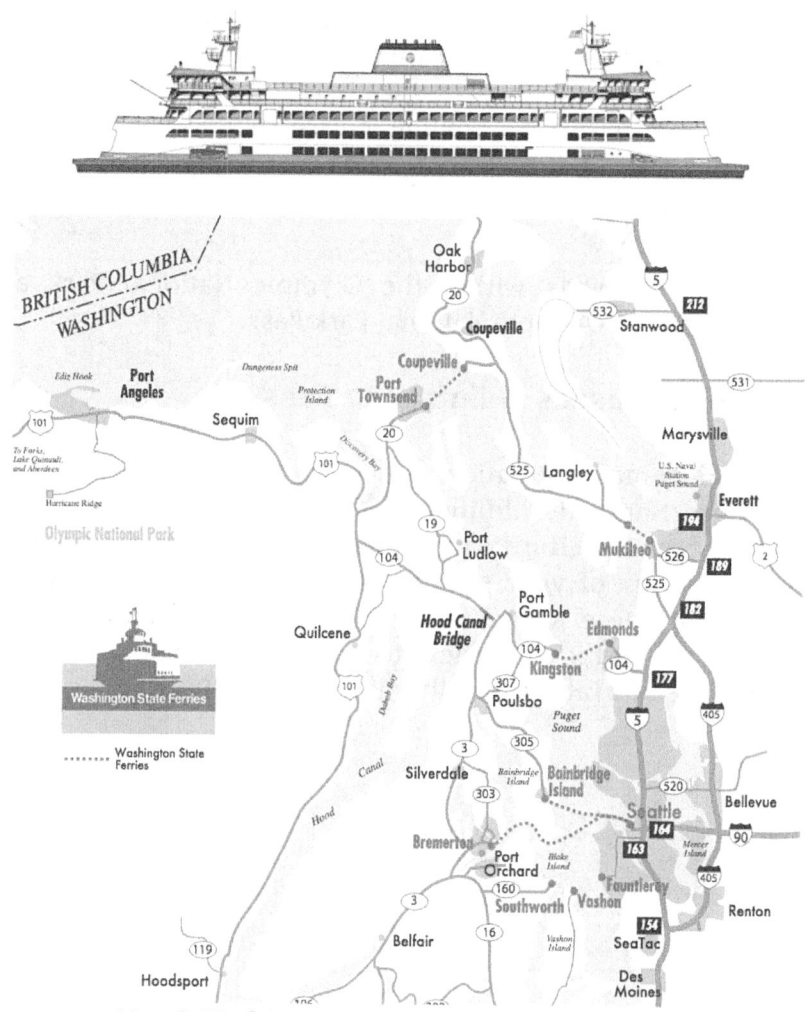

Map © Washington State Dept. of Transportation

Due to its vast size, you'll need to explore the northern Olympic Peninsula by car, especially its western areas and destinations. To reach the peninsula, you have two choices; you may either drive all the way there, or you may take a ferry for a portion of your drive from Seattle, Edmonds or Coupeville. Each ferry takes you to a different point from which to begin your exploration of the peninsula.

Driving to the Northern Peninsula

The northern Olympic Peninsula may be reached via driving north along Hwy 101 from Olympia and following this along Hood Canal on the western shores of Puget Sound, or via Highway 16 and Hwy 3 northwest out of Tacoma, taking you through Bremerton and Port Gamble.

Taking a Ferry to the Northern Olympic Peninsula

If you do not wish to drive all the way down to the southern end of Puget Sound / Olympia / Tacoma before driving back north to the northern Olympic Peninsula, then you may cross Puget Sound via a ferryboat at Coupeville, Edmonds, or Seattle.

Coupeville to Port Townsend Ferry

Located north of Seattle, the small town of Coupeville offers a ferry that takes you to Port Townsend on the northeast tip of the northern Olympic Peninsula. Note, however, that though Coupeville is approximately 60 miles north of Seattle, one must drive a circuitous 103 mile route from Seattle to reach Coupeville, or take the Mukilteo ferry as part of a 60 mile drive. As a result, the Coupeville to Port Townsend ferry is a good option only if you are coming from the north.

Coupeville Ferry Terminal
1400 WA-20
Coupeville, WA 98239

Edmonds to Kingston Ferry

Edmonds is located approximately 17 miles north of Seattle. From the Edmonds ferry terminal, take the short ferry ride across Puget Sound to the town of Kingston on Bainbridge Island. From here, follow Hwy 104 northwest across the Hood Canal Floating Bridge the northern Olympic Peninsula.

From Everett and Points North and East

Drive SOUTH on Interstate 5 to State Route (SR) 104, taking Exit 177. Continue WEST on SR 104 for 4 miles and follow the signs to the Edmonds Ferry Terminal.

From Seattle and Points South

Drive NORTH on Interstate 5 to State Route (SR) 104, taking Exit 177. Continue WEST on SR 104 for 4 miles and follow the signs to the Edmonds Ferry Terminal. Vehicles must enter the tollbooths at SR 104 & Dayton Avenue via SR 104 northbound, but not from Dayton Street.

Edmonds to Kingston Ferry Terminal
199 Sunset Ave. South
Edmonds, WA 98020

Seattle to Bainbridge Island Ferry

The Seattle to Bainbridge Island Ferry leaves from the downtown Seattle Waterfront and crosses Puget Sound to Bainbridge Island. From here, follow Hwy 305 north through Poulsbo and then across the Hood Canal Bridge to Hwy 104 or Hwy 19 to the northern Olympic Peninsula.

The ferry across Puget Sound takes 45 minutes to 1 hour. Plan on arriving at the ferry terminal in Seattle one hour in advance. There is a good deal of road construction going on at the Seattle waterfront, and it is easy to take a wrong turn as your onboard navigator tries its best to determine what kind of traffic changes have occurred in just the last week. Leave yourself plenty of time for a few wrong turns, a circle or two around the block(s), and just simply getting off route before reaching your destination.

Seattle to Bainbridge Island Ferry Terminal
801 Alaskan Way Pier 52
Seattle, WA 98104

From I-5 Northbound

- Take Exit 164B for Edgar Martinez Drive South
- Turn right onto Edgar Martinez Drive South
- Turn right onto 1st Avenue South / Dave Niehaus Way South (You're now heading north)
- Slight left onto Railroad Way South / SR 519
- Continue north to follow SR 519
- Turn left on Jackson Street to access the terminal
- Note that these directions may change due to road construction

Note: As you approach Seattle from the south, your onboard / onphone navigator *may* direct you to take Hwy 99 instead of I-5 North into the Seattle area so as to save time due to traffic congestion on I-5. This will work well, but be advised that once you begin to reach downtown Seattle, your onboard navigator *may* then tell you to be in the "second from the right" lane when taking the exit from Hwy 99 to Alaskan Way and the Seattle waterfront. *This is incorrect.* With Seattle's new tunnel project, you will want to be in the *far right* lane when taking this exit. If you are in the second from the right lane, you will then enter the tunnel and will not be able to exit for some time. Once you exit the tunnel, you will then need to work your way back south through Seattle to the waterfront / Jackson Street and the ferry terminal. *Don't forget...if you miss your ferry, there will be another one coming along soon, so don't worry about it.* Note that once you exit from Hwy 99 onto Alaskan Way, you will continue to Jackson Street, where you'll turn left to access the ferry terminal.

From I-5 Southbound

- Use the right 2 lanes to take Exit 164 to Interstate 90 East toward Bellevue / Spokane. This may seem counter intuitive, but go ahead and take this exit
- Use the right lane to keep right at the fork and now follow the signs for Interstate 5 South / Tacoma / Portland, instead of Bellevue / Spokane. You do not want to continue on toward Tacoma / Portland, but instead will soon be taking the exit for 4th Avenue South
- Keep right at the fork and follow the signs for 4th Avenue South / Ferries
- Then keep left at the fork and follow the signs for E Martinez Drive
- Use any lane to turn right onto Edgar Martinez Drive South
- Turn right onto 1st Avenue South / Dave Niehaus Way South (You're now heading north)
- Slight left onto Railroad Way South / SR 519
- Continue north to follow SR 519
- Turn left on Jackson Street to access the terminal
- Note that these directions may change due to road construction

"Ferry Important" Things to Know

Fare Information

Your fare to ride the ferry covers your car and the driver. You will need to pay one additional "Passenger Fare" for each additional person in your car.

You may pay for a one-way or round-trip ticket, depending upon the departure terminal.

22

You may buy your fares online, and this will save you some time when you drive up to the entrance kiosk. Be sure to bring your paperwork with you. That said, purchasing your fares at the kiosk goes quickly.

Single, full-fare tickets for both passengers and a driver and vehicle may be purchased online with a credit card at www.wsdot.wa.gov/ferries/wave2go/ and printed at home up to 90 days in advance of your travel date.

Fares are based upon which ferry route you are taking and the length, width, and height of your vehicle. Discounts are also provided based upon age and any disabilities. Note that seniors, persons with disabilities and passengers with a Medicare card or other eligibility verification are eligible for travel at half the regular passenger fare rate.

Boarding the Ferry

Once you buy or present a ticket, you will be directed to pull your car forward on the dock and wait in a numbered lane until the ferry arrives. Once the ferry unloads its load of cars, motorcyclists, bike riders, and passengers, you will be directed by personnel to drive your car to an assigned area aboard the ferry. The ferries can easily accommodate vehicles up to 7'2" in height or 22' in length. Vehicles that exceed these limits may be loaded out of sequence and subject to a surcharge.

Departure Times

Ferries from Seattle *to* Bainbridge Island and Edmonds *to* Kingston begin sailing early in the morning, at approximately 5:30 a.m. Ferries depart *approximately* every 50 minutes to an hour throughout the day until late into the night. Ferries departing *from* Bainbridge Island and Kingston follow a similar schedule, with ferries sailing beginning at 4:45 a.m. Note that weekday departure times vary a bit from weekend departure times.

Ferries from Coupeville to Port Townsend begin leaving nearly two hours later than the Seattle and Edmonds ferries, and they depart roughly every 1.5 hours.

For the latest ferry departure and arrival times, visit www.wsdot.wa.gov/ferries/schedule

Note: As a general rule, it is recommended that you arrive at your ferry terminal at least 1 hour before your departure time.

Seattle Ferry Terminal Road Construction

There is a good chance you will encounter road construction when driving to the ferry terminal on the Seattle waterfront. Expect minor delays and routes that may or may not match your onboard navigation.

Don't Worry

If you miss your preferred ferry for whatever reason, do not worry, as there will be another ferry along in a little while.

Seattle Traffic

Note that traffic in Seattle is usually often and slow, so plan on needing extra time to reach your destination.

A Review Would Be Very Helpful

If your daily schedule isn't too hectic after you get back home from all of the fun adventures awaiting you on the Olympic Peninsula, we'd certainly appreciate it if you could take a moment to leave a review for this book online. You see, reviews go a long way toward helping us create guidebooks such as the *Northern Olympic Peninsula – An Explorer's Guide*, and better yet, they help encourage others to set out on their own adventures, whatever and wherever they may be.

www.Discover-Washington.com

Point Wilson Lighthouse

Port Gamble
&
Port Townsend

PORT GAMBLE

If you take either the Seattle to Bainbridge Island or Edmonds to Kingston ferry to the Olympic Peninsula, you will be passing close to the small town of Port Gamble when approaching the Hood Canal Floating Bridge. Host to retail shops, restaurants, lodging, a museum, beautiful water views, and more, this quaint "company town" is filled with turn-of-the-century buildings and historic homes featuring impressive New England style architecture. Be sure to stop here for a meal and to take a stroll as you learn all about Port Gamble's colorful history tied to saw mills and shipping.

 ☐ **State Champion Camperdown Elm**

Port Townsend is home to an impressive State Champion tree. Unlike the towering Sitka spruce or Douglas Fir champions you'll find elsewhere, this is a Camperdown Elm. Its unique trunk twists and turns to a height of 20', while its crown weighs in at 26' wide. What is even more impressive is that while it is a champion tree, it cannot self reproduce, as Camperdown Elms must be grafted to a Scotch Elm in order to grow, and as such need the skilled hands of an arborist to keep it alive as a species.

Follow the long pathway immediately south of the Port Townsend General Store and look to the south. There you will find Port Townsend's Camperdown Elm.

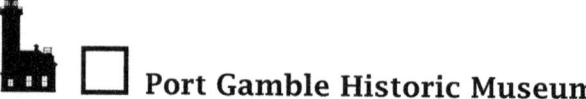 Port Gamble Historic Museum

 Established as a company mill town in 1853 by William Talbot and Andrew Pope, Port Gamble was a small community centered around a busy sawmill that worked continuously until 1995 to provide lumber for the San Francisco market and cities around the world.

Step into the Port Gamble Historic Museum to learn all about the interesting history of this small town with it's quaint New England style architecture.

Admission:

    Adults: $4.00
    Students / Seniors / Military: $3.00
    Children (6 and Under): Free

Port Gamble Historic Museum
32400 N Rainier Ave.
Port Gamble, WA 98364
360-297-8078

- Open Memorial Day Weekend to Labor Day Weekend - Friday through Sunday - 12:00 p.m. to 5:00 p.m. -

www.Discover-Washington.com

Port Townsend

Located at the northeastern tip of the Olympic Peninsula, Port Townsend was the center of nearly all ocean-going trade in the northwest during the latter half of the 1800s. Over 1,000 sailing vessels from around the world would call on this bustling seaport every year, transferring their cargo to a smaller "Mosquito Fleet" of vessels that would then ply the waters of Puget Sound, a tight archipelago of difficult to navigate islands and peninsulas. Soon, Port Townsend grew to become the "New York of the West", where wooden structures gave way to stately stone and brick buildings housing government officials, foreign consulates, grand hotels, and oft-visited businesses of ill repute. Riches made on the docks, legal and otherwise, were spent on fine Victorian homes high on the bluff above town, many of which still stand.

Today, Port Townsend greets visitors with a rich maritime heritage, a vibrant waterfront, and a welcoming spirit.

Note: To make your life much easier, be sure to be in the left lane when entering the historic downtown section of Port Townsend on Water Street. The right hand lane somewhat abruptly terminates at the ferry terminal entrance as you enter the downtown area, and this can be a bit confusing as you suddenly find yourself having to navigate a lane change in the middle of an intersection.

www.Discover-Washington.com

 **Finnriver Farm & Cidery**

In addition to offering an impressive selection of traditional and contemporary ciders, dessert wines, special releases, and more, all crafted from the 80 acres of organic fields and orchards on site, Finnriver Farm & Cidery offers visitors a varied menu of delicious hot meals made with locally sourced ingredients, all in a welcoming country setting that doubles as a wildlife sanctuary. As a result, expect to see deer, rabbits, eagles, perhaps an owl or two, and a lot of geese! (Note: Please keep your dog in your car while visiting.)

Finnriver Farm & Cidery
124 Center Road
Chimacum, WA 98325
360-339-8478

- Open: Daily – 12:00 p.m. to 9:00 p.m.

 **Northwest School of Wooden Boat Building**

It's hard to decide what is more impressive at the Northwest School of Boat Building, the fine craftsmanship that goes into the hand-crafted construction of every wooden vessel or the passion with which it occurs.

Located off of Hwy 19 and scattered among many different buildings is the Heritage Campus of the accredited Northwest School of Boat Building. Looking nothing like a typical school, behind its many doors you'll find students of all ages and abilities learning and practicing this historical maritime craft, which is so important to the Puget Sound region today.

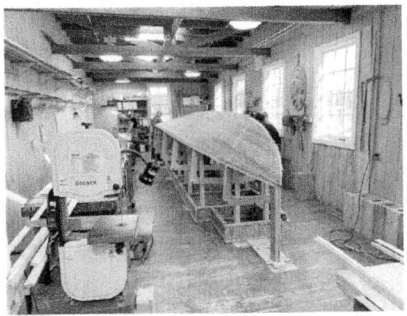

Visitors are more than welcome to stop by and take a look anytime, and self-guided walking tours of the school are offered at 3:30 p.m. on the first Friday of every month. Stop in at the Administration Office to sign up for the tour, pick up a map, and then move from building to building at your own pace as you see firsthand how the art, science, and tradition of craftsmanship continues today at the Northwest School of Boat Building.

Note that all visitors must check in at the Administration Office before entering any shops or taking any photos, be it when taking a tour or also just stopping by.

> Northwest School of Boat Building
> Administration Building
> 42 North Water Street
> Port Hadlock, WA 98339
> 360-385-4948

- Open: Monday – 9:00 a.m. to 5:00 p.m. – Tuesday through Friday – 8:00 a.m. to 5:00 p.m.

Note that the **Ajax Café** across the street is a popular destination with the locals.

www.Discover-Washington.com

 Port Townsend Aero Museum

Step out of your car and into the wild blue yonder at the Port Townsend Aero Museum. Here, a growing collection of beautifully restored antique aircraft, all of which can fly, are on display in a modern hangar museum.

Stroll among a Rose Parakeet Biplane, a Corben "Baby Ace", a 1937 Beech C17B "Staggerwing", a 1942 PT-17 Stearman Kaydet, and many, many other vintage aircraft, all under the responsibility of a corps of teenagers who have been given job skills training as they learn to restore, maintain and even fly these impressive planes. As you make your way through the museum you'll want to be sure to visit the walkway on the second level for another perspective.

Note that the museum, with its mission to provide opportunities for teenaged youth, is a publicly owned non-profit entity that receives no tax-based funding. As a result, all donations to the program are greatly appreciated and may be made at the museum or through their website.

    Port Townsend Aero Museum
    105 Airport Road
    Port Townsend, WA 98368
    360-379-5244

- Open: Wednesday – Sunday – 9:00 a.m. to 4:00 p.m.

Admission:

    Adults: $10.00
    Seniors: $9.00
    Active Military: $9.00
    Youth (7-12): $6.00
    Children (6 and under): Free

 ## ☐ Port Townsend Foundry

Though it has been in operation since 1983, the small Port Townsend Foundry has a history that reaches back to the late 1800s, as it supplied many of the facades and other architectural features adorning the buildings of early Port Townsend. Today, it designs, tools, pours, and finishes over 6,000 different non-ferrous items that are used around the world, from architectural elements to maritime hardware.

Stop in and meet the owners, Pete and Susan, and ask for a tour of the place. Call ahead and you may even be able to arrange to be there during the days of the week on which they do pourings. Note that it is best if you stop by after 9:00 a.m. and before 4:30 p.m., Tuesday through Friday. Tours are not scheduled, but walk-ins are welcome. Visitors are also welcome to call or email ahead of their visit to set a date and time.

    Port Townsend Foundry
    251 Otto Street
    Port Townsend, WA 98368
    360-385-6425
    PTF@Olypen.com

- Open: Monday through Friday – 8:00 a.m. to 5:00 p.m.

☐ Redfish Custom Wood Kayak & Canoe Co.

One of our favorite experiences when on a road trip is to walk into a nondescript building and find works of art "hidden" inside. That's certainly the case with Redfish Custom Wood Kayak & Canoe Company. Open the door at 153 Otto Street, step inside, and you'll immediately be immersed in the world of fine handcrafted wood strip kayaks, canoes, and paddleboards. Vessels in various states of construction fill the space, while finished kayaks are showcased nearby, each a masterful work of art. Feel free to purchase a kayak or sign up for a class to make your own!

Visitors are more than welcome to stop by and meet the owner, Joe Greenley, as well as take a look around, marvel at the fine craftsmanship, and ask questions.

Redfish Custom Kayak & Canoe Co.
153 Otto Street - Suite G
Port Townsend, WA 98368
360-808-5488

- Open: Monday through Friday - 9:00 a.m. to 9:00 p.m.

www.Discover-Washington.com

 **Massey Copper**

Step into the small shop of master coppersmith Walter Massey and you'll be surrounded by not only the equipment and tools of his craft, but also beautiful works of custom hand-forged copper art reflecting the beauty and wildlife of the Olympic Peninsula, as well as garden sculptures, architectural pieces, and perhaps even a Viking ship!

    Massey Copper
    1431 Irondale Rd.
    Port Hadlock, WA 98339
    360-344-3611

Open: It is best to call beforehand to schedule your visit.

 Port Townsend Walking Tour

Hear tales of the men and women who persevered to build a small town that would grow to become the "New York of the west", a bustling Victorian seaport that welcomed a never-ending parade of tall sailing vessels from around the world, and the soaring fortunes, colorful characters, disreputable businesses, and impressive architecture that came with them. Learn how it all came to an end with the advent of steamships, and how Port Townsend soon faded away...only to be revived again.

"Downtown" walking tours occur during Saturdays at 2:00 p.m. from June through September and last approximately 1 hour. Expect to walk about one-half mile. Reservations are required and may be made by calling 360-385-1003 at least 48 hours in advance of your preferred tour date, or online at www.JCHSMuseum.org/programs/WalkingTours. (Note that last-minute spots may be available from time to time.) Tickets are $15.00 per person, $5.00 for children ages 5 to 18. Meet 15 minutes prior to the scheduled departure time at the Jefferson Museum of Art & History, located at 540 Water Street, Port Townsend, WA 98368. (Photo)

For those who are interested in the Victorian architecture of the fine homes and churches on the bluff above Port Townsend, you may wish to choose the "Uptown Tour" option.

 ☐ **Port Townsend Visitor Center**

Want to learn more about Port Townsend first-hand? Then stop in at the Visitor Center to visit with the friendly staff, see what events are occurring while you're in town, and to learn a tip or two about the area.

Port Townsend Visitor Center
2409 Jefferson Street
Port Townsend, WA 98368
360-385-2722

- Open:
  - Monday – Friday: 9:00 a.m. to 5:00 p.m.
  - Saturday: 10:00 a.m. to 4:00 p.m.
  - Sunday: 11:00 a.m. to 4:00 p.m.

 ☐ Kelly Art Deco Light Museum

Simply put, there's nothing like this one-of-a-kind museum. If you appreciate fine Art Deco design, then you'll want to make your way to the Kelly Art Deco Light Museum. Located upstairs at Custom Reproduction Lighting, and methodically showcased on display, are over 400 rare authentic chandeliers, wall sconces, table lights and more from the years of 1928 to 1938 that "graced the homes of that exciting time in America's history when gangsters ran the streets, speak-easies were common, and formerly rich businessmen sold apples on corners for a penny." Admission is free.

Custom Reproduction Lighting
Kelly Art Deco Light Museum
200 West Sims Way
Port Townsend, WA 98368
360-379-9030

- Open: Monday through Saturday – 10:00 a.m. to 5:00 p.m.

www.Discover-Washington.com

 ## LaughinGnome Pottery Studio

We discovered LaughinGnome Pottery while enjoying the Port Townsend Art Walk one Saturday evening. As you hold their work in your hand you get a sense of the creativity, passion and pride that goes into each piece carefully handcrafted from the rich red clay of the Ohio River Valley. If you were to drink from one of their mugs, cups or other vessels, you would discover that this clay gives the piece a "magical" quality that significantly enhances the flavor of whatever you're drinking. According to the Laughing Gnome... *"The rough surface of our unglazed cup has microscopic pockets, or holes, that trap molecules of oxygen. This is called nucleation. Nucleation brings out the flavor and aroma compounds of coffee, tea, wine, spirits, etc. so they are more available to our taste and smell."*

Stop in at their studio to see them at work and to peruse the many home, kitchen, and garden pieces they offer for sale.

LaughinGnome Pottery Studio
2009 4th Street, Ste B
Port Townsend, WA 98368
360-301-5646

- Open: Monday through Friday – 12:00 p.m. to 5:00 p.m. You'll also find LaughinGnome Pottery at the Port Townsend Farmers Market, located in uptown Port Townsend. Learn more on page 60.

www.Discover-Washington.com

 Blue Moose Cafe

Plan to wait a while for breakfast, (and lunch) as the Blue Moose Café is usually busy. Locals and visitors alike fill the handful of tables and counter seats as they savor classic breakfast fare served with a creative and delicious twist. Look for it amid the boats of the Port Townsend Boat Haven / Marina.

Blue Moose Café
Port Townsend Boat Haven / Marina
311 Haines Place
Port Townsend, WA 98368
360-385-7339

- Open: Monday through Friday – 6:30 a.m. to 2:00 p.m., Saturday and Sunday – 7:00 a.m. to 2:00 p.m.

 Port Townsend Boat Haven / Marina

After having breakfast at the Blue Moose Café, take some time to walk the docks and see an interesting collection of fishing trawlers and pleasure craft up close, some of which are classic works of art, such as the 1927 Wells Gray, winner of the "Best Power Restoration Award – Victoria Classic Boat Show". (Photo) Afterwards, stroll a while along the nearby Larry Scott Trail heading southwest on the waterfront.

Port Townsend Boat Haven
2790 Washington Street
Port Townsend, WA 98368
360-385-2355

- Open: Monday through Saturday – 8:00 a.m. to 4:30 p.m.

 ☐ **John Steinbeck's Western Flyer**

In 1940, Noble and Pulitzer Prize winning author John Steinbeck embarked on an expedition with his friend, marine biologist Ed Ricketts, to the Sea of Cortez in the Gulf of California aboard the boat *Western Flyer*. Here, they spent six weeks collecting and studying marine specimens, which resulted in the publication of one of Steinbeck's most important works, *The Log from the Sea of Cortez*. Today, the *Western Flyer* is regarded by many as "the most famous fishing vessel ever to have sailed."

After sinking twice and having fallen into a state of significant disrepair, the Western Flyer now resides inside a non-descript building in the Port Townsend Boat Haven, where it is undergoing an expensive and time-consuming restoration with the intent that future generations of students will be inspired by the work of Steinbeck and Ricketts to pursue careers in both literature and science.

Look for the *Western Flyer* inside the Port Townsend Shipwrights Co-op building, directly across from the Blue Moose Café. (Photo)

Port Townsend Shipwrights Co-op
919 Haines Place
Port Townsend, WA 98368
360-385-6138

- Open: Monday through Friday – 8:00 a.m. to 5:00 p.m.

 ☐ **Larry Scott Trail**

Making up the eastern end of the 130-mile Olympic Discovery Trail, the Larry Scott Trail is a "rails to trails" path that traverses west for 7.3 miles from the Port Townsend Boat Haven to the Milo Curry Trailhead. Open to non-motorized transportation, it makes for a nice walk along the waterfront.

Directions: Turn south off of West Simms Way onto Haines Place (Opposite the Safeway store) and follow this as it makes its way past the Blue Moose Café to the waterfront. You'll see the trailhead as you approach the water.

Note that you may rent a bike to ride on the Larry Scott Trail from **The Broken Spoke,** Port Townsend's Premier Bicycle Shop.

The Broken Spoke
630 Water Street
Port Townsend, WA 98368
360-379-1295

- Open: Monday through Saturday – 10:00 a.m. to 6:00 p.m., Sunday – 11:00 a.m. to 4:00 p.m.

☐ Dimick Lighthouse

Located approximately 35 miles southeast of Port Townsend, across Puget Sound, is the Mukilteo Lighthouse. A stately wooden structure built in 1906 that today still guides ships, but also serves as a museum. High on a bluff in Port Townsend is the Dimick Lighthouse. Built in 1990, it is a near exact replica of the Mukilteo Lighthouse and serves as the vacation home of the Dimick family. *Note that it is a private residence and is not open to the public.* To get a good look at the lighthouse, visit the sidewalk in front of the Old Consulate Inn. (Page 151)

Dimick Lighthouse
1935 Washington Street
Port Townsend, WA 98368

 ☐ Jefferson County Courthouse

Built in the Romanesque style in 1892 and today housing government offices, the Jefferson County Courthouse captures your attention with its impressive architecture, stone and brick façade, and commanding presence. Towering over it all is a 124'  high bell tower that rings on the hour and can be heard for miles around. If you're there near the top of the hour, be sure to wait for it.

Jefferson County Courthouse
1820 Jefferson Street
Port Townsend, WA 98368
360-385-9360

☐ Hike the Historic Downtown Waterfront – Water Street

What was once the business district of a bustling sea port housing banks, shipwrights, mercantiles, a jail, and numerous bars, hotels, and businesses of ill-repute, today hosts a vast collection of shops, boutiques, galleries, museums, boat builders, theatres, restaurants, historic hotels, and more, all in well-preserved 120 year-old Victorian-era buildings, many of which are listed on the National Register of Historic Places.

Be sure to take the time to stroll along Water Street, from the ferry terminal to the Point Hudson Marina, to peruse its many shops, enjoy a meal, take in a show, and perhaps catch one of the many festival events which occur throughout each year.

www.Discover-Washington.com

 ☐ **Hastings Building**

There are a number of impressive Victorian-era buildings on Water Street in Port Townsend, and one which captures many visitors' attention is the 1890 Hastings Building, an elegant structure with an Italianate façade that retains much of its original 130 year-old architectural features, including a 4th floor turret room, a wrought iron widow's walk, redwood wainscoting and its original hardware.

Hastings Building
839 Water Street
Port Townsend, WA 98368
206-387-9846

 ☐ **Port Townsend Chocolates**

We always like to include outstanding local chocolatiers in our guides, and our choice in Port Townsend is...the Port Townsend Chocolate Company, where "*Every Bite is a Small Vacation!*" Step into Lehani's Deli and Coffee and find an abundance of chocolate choices in the showcase up front, including truffles, chocolate bars, creamy fudge, chocolate covered caramels, and much more. You'll want to enjoy a fresh pastry, bowl of soup, and cup of hot coffee while you're in the deli, too.

Port Townsend Chocolate Company/
Lehani's Deli and Coffee
221 Taylor Street
Port Townsend, WA 98368
360-385-3961

- Open:
  - Monday through Thursday – 8:00 a.m. to 4:00 p.m.
  - Friday – 8:00 a.m. to 5:00 p.m.
  - Saturday – 9:00 a.m. to 5:00 p.m.
  - Sunday – 10:00 a.m. to 4:00 p.m.

☐ Rothschild House Museum

Located on a bluff overlooking Port Townsend is the 1868 Rothschild House Museum. Managed by the Jefferson Museum of Art & History, this simple historic structure may not reflect the architectural detail of its Victorian-era counterparts nearby, but it provides perhaps the most accurate portrayal of life in Port Townsend over 100 years ago. The home was owned and occupied through the years by only the Rothschild family, and the last surviving family member donated it to the Washington State Parks and Recreation Commission, which opened it as a historic site in 1962. The home was left intact and each of its rooms were restored to period-specific detail reflecting life as the Rothschild family lived it during the late 1800s to early 1900s. *Photo © Jefferson County Historical Society*

Admission:

Note that a 3-Museum pass to the Rothschild House Museum, Commanding Officer's Quarters Museum at Fort Worden, and the Jefferson Museum of Art & History is available here at a discounted rate. The following rates are for the Rothschild House only.

Adults: $6.00
Seniors: $5.00
Children: $1.00

Rothschild House Museum
418 Taylor Street
Port Townsend, WA 98368
360-385-1003

- Open: Daily – 11:00 a.m. to 4:00 p.m. – May through September

 ## St. Paul's Episcopal Church

Within Port Townsend's Uptown area one can find many impressive homes with Victorian-era architecture and details. Scattered amongst these homes are a handful of churches, one of which is the beautiful 1865 St. Paul's Episcopal Church. Built in the Gothic Revival style featuring pointed arches, a steeply pitched roof, and delicate trim work, it is an active church and still holds regular services.

Note that St. Paul's Episcopal Church is located a little over one block south of the Rothschild House Museum.

St. Paul's Episcopal Church
1020 Jefferson Street
Port Townsend, WA 98368
360-385-0770

 ☐ **Historical Fire Bell Tower**

In the late 1800s, many of the buildings in Port Townsend were built of wood and used gas flame lamps, lanterns, and at times candles for lighting. As a result, they were susceptible to fire, and if one should ever get out of control, the results could be devastating, especially amongst the tightly packed wooden structures of the waterfront.

In 1890, Port Townsend constructed a 75' tall wooden bell tower high on the bluff above the city and installed a 1,500 pound brass bell, which, using a coded pattern of ringing, was used to call volunteer firefighters to action and direct them to the scene. This "Fire Bell Tower" was used for more than 50 years before being replaced by newer technologies, but today the tower still stands, restored and maintained as a link to Port Townsend's colorful history.

Note that this is the only remaining fire bell tower in the United States.

Historical Fire Bell Tower
319 Tyler Street
Port Townsend, WA 98368
360-385-1003

www.Discover-Washington.com

 The Rose Theatre

We're fans of the history of the northwest, so what better place to see high-quality plays, live music, first-run films, and more when you're in Port Townsend than the historic 1907 Rose Theatre? Arrive early and be sure to make your way to the small balcony to see your performance!

The Rose Theatre
235 Taylor Street
Port Townsend, WA 98368
360-385-1089 (Movie Hotline)

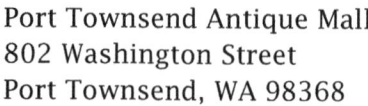 Port Townsend Antique Mall

If you like antiques, then you're sure to like the Port Townsend Antique Mall. Here, countless stalls upstairs and down are filled with an interesting and vast collection of well-curated antiques covering many different eras and subjects.

Port Townsend Antique Mall
802 Washington Street
Port Townsend, WA 98368

- Open:
    - Monday through Friday – 10:30 a.m. to 5:30 p.m.
    - Saturday – 10:30 a.m. to 6:00 p.m.
    - Sunday – 11:00 a.m. to 5:00 p.m.

 ## Bergstrom's Antique & Classic Autos

If it has to do with antique cars, then you'll find it at Bergstrom's Antique & Classic Autos. Step inside this 1917 garage and discover an abundance of antiques and vintage items all relating to the cars of yesteryear. Spare parts, car manuals, garage signs, light bulbs, posters, gas pumps, hub caps, toy cars and trucks, and even some classic automobiles are all for sale.

Bergstrom's Antique & Classic Autos
809 Washington Street
Port Townsend, WA 98368
360-385-5061

Open:

- Monday – 10:00 a.m. to 5:00 p.m.
- Thursday through Saturday – 10:00 a.m. to 5:00 p.m.
- Closed Tuesday, Wednesday and Sunday

www.Discover-Washington.com

 ☐ **Elevated Ice Cream & Candy Shop**

Take a moment in your day to enjoy some fresh homemade ice cream, sherbet, and non-dairy Italian ices, which are made in 30 different flavors on site at the old-fashioned Elevated Ice Cream shop on Water Street. Then step next door to the Candy Shop and pick up some delicious chocolates, truffles and fudge to enjoy as you walk about town.

> Elevated Ice Cream & Candy Shop
> 627 & 631 Water Street
> Port Townsend, WA 98368
> 360-385-1156

Open:

- Friday through Saturday – 10:00 a.m. to 10:00 p.m.
- Sunday through Thursday – 10:00 a.m. to 6:00 p.m.

 ☐ **Jefferson Museum of Art & History**

During your trip to Port Townsend, you'll have the opportunity to visit three unique museums, all under the management of the Jefferson County Historical Society; the Rothschild House Museum, the Commanding Officer's Quarters at Fort Worden State

Park, and the Jefferson Museum of Art & History. Combined, all three provide an excellent overview of the cultural, historical, geographical, economical, and military history of the area.

Step inside the Jefferson Museum of Art & History, which used to be the local courthouse and jail, and make your way back to 1892, when life in Port Townsend was very rough around the edges and good use was often made of the sturdy iron bar jail downstairs. Go ahead and close the door to the jail, but rest assured you're still free to peruse the exhibits upstairs that reveal the history and daily life of Port Townsend.

Admission:

> Note that a 3-Museum pass to the Jefferson Museum of Art & History, Commanding Officer's Quarters Museum at Fort Worden, and the Rothschild House Museum is available here at a discounted rate. The following rates are for the Jefferson Museum of Art & History only.
>
> Adults: $6.00
> Seniors: $5.00
> Children: $1.00
>
> Jefferson Museum of Art & History
> 540 Water Street
> Port Townsend, WA 98368
> 360-385-1003

Open:

- Wednesday though Monday – 11:00 a.m. to 4:00 p.m.

High Tea at Café Tenby

Add a touch of class to your trip by partaking of "High Tea" at Café Tenby on Water Street, featuring Pippa's Real Tea. Rated one of the Top 5 Tea Rooms in Western Washington, and *Best Tea House* in the Seattle Region, Café Tenby takes on an air of royalty every Saturday at 12:00 p.m. and 2:00 p.m., plus Sundays at 12:00 p.m., as it serves guests delectable tea sandwiches and fresh baked pastries, seasonal fruit, and delicious scones served with clotted cream. Reservations are required and may be made online at www.CafeTenby.com or by calling 360-385-6060.

Two tea services are available; High Tea - $42.00 per person, and Royal High Tea with a glass of bubbly - $52.00 per person. Both services have in addition a 15% service charge plus tax.

If you can't make High Tea, then by all means stop in anytime and enjoy freshly made loose leaf teas brewed to perfection, proper scones with real clotted cream, warm seasonal soups, assorted baked goods and pastries, and delicious sandwiches, all in a comfortable welcoming setting.

Be sure to ask about their "High Tea Picnic", perfect for taking with you, and do remember to visit the beautiful courtyard garden in back.

So, What is Clotted Cream?

According the Café Tenby's web site...There is only one ingredient in clotted cream: cream.

Clotted Cream is cooked for a very long time at a very low heat, and then it has to set up for 24 hours. It becomes a luscious, thick, glorious topping for Café Tenby's English scones and jam. We use organic cream from local dairies, and the result has been compared to the best that Cornwall or Devon, England have to offer.

Café Tenby
636 Water Street
Port Townsend, WA 98368
360-385-6060

Open:

- Wednesday through Saturday – 9:00 a.m. to 4:00 p.m.
- Sunday – 9:00 a.m. to 2:30 p.m.

 Northwest Maritime Center

Located at the northeast end of Water Street, next to Point Hudson Marina and overlooking Puget Sound, is the large Northwest Maritime Center. Comprised of a campus of buildings, its mission is "to engage and educate people of all generations in traditional and contemporary maritime life, in a spirit of adventure and discovery." Here, students learn about sailing, the essentials of safe navigation, how to understand radar and night piloting, the effects of coastal winds, proper outboard maintenance, the role of tides and currents, northwest weather, and much more. The center also sponsors international sailing trips, the adventurous Race to Alaska, and the very popular Port Townsend Wooden Boat Festival. (Pg. 61)

In addition, the Northwest Maritime Center is home to The Wooden Boat Foundation Boat Shop. You're more than welcome to step inside and get an up close look at the boat building process as student craftsmen learn and practice the time-honored skills passed down from generation to generation of boat builders. Be sure to take the steps to the walkway above for an interesting overhead view.

Note: If it's a bit breezy during your visit to Port Townsend, or if you'd like to find a quiet spot with a nice view of Puget Sound, then make your way to the upper deck on the east side of the Northwest Maritime Center. Here, you'll find a few benches tucked out of the way but in the sun. It's a great spot to enjoy an early morning coffee.

    Northwest Maritime Center
    431 Water Street
    Port Townsend, WA 98368
    360-385-3628

- Open: Daily – 9:00 a.m. to 5:00 p.m., though these hours can vary depending upon the availability of volunteers.

www.Discover-Washington.com

 ☐ **Whale Watching – Puget Sound Express**

 The Olympic Peninsula affords many opportunities to see orcas, gray whales, humpbacks, and more from shore, and the sight of these magnificent animals is simply breathtaking, even from a distance. However, if you'd like to see them much closer, from out on the water instead of from the water's edge, then we highly recommend you enjoy a whale watching tour.

Puget Sound Express provides three whale watching tours out of Port Townsend:

Gray Whale Tours – 3 to 4 Hours - Early March to Late April

Every spring, majestic gray whales migrate with their newborn calves along the Pacific coastline from the warm waters of Mexico up to Alaska and the Bering Sea, where they feed for the summer months before beginning their migration back south. During March and April, they enter the Strait of Juan de Fuca and Puget Sound as part of their journey north, and this gives you an opportunity to see them up close.

- Leave Port Townsend at 10:00 a.m. – 3 to 4 Hour tour
- Adults: $85 – Children (2-10): $65 – Infants: Free
- Check in 45 minutes prior to departure.
- Call prior to your arrival to check the dates available for your trip and to receive additional details.

Port Townsend Whale Watching Tour – 4 Hours - Late April to Late October

Journey from Port Townsend into the cool waters of the Salish Sea as you spend 4 hours spotting gray whales, tufted puffins, California and Steller sea lions, bald eagles and more, all as a trained marine naturalist gladly answers any questions you may have.

- The 4 hour tour leaves Port Townsend at 10:00 a.m. (April – October) and 2:30 p.m. (June – Early Sept.)
- Large 40-seat tour boat
- Indoor seating with a wrap-around viewing deck, snack bar and restroom
- Adults: $95 – Children (2-10): $65 – Infants: Free
- Check in 45 minutes prior to your departure time.
- Call prior to your arrival to check dates available for your trip and to receive additional details.
- Note that you have the option of preordering a gourmet box lunch from The Courtyard Café in Port Townsend. (360-379-3355) All orders must be placed by at least 3:00 p.m. the day before your tour.

Port Townsend San Juan Island Whale Watching Tour – 8 Hours - Early May to Late September

For those with a bit more time in their schedule, the Port Townsend San Juan Island Whale Watching tour is just the adventure. You'll depart Port Townsend at 9:00 a.m. and make your way along the official ferry route to Friday Harbor on San Juan Island while watching for minke whales, gray whales, humpbacks, sea lions, eagles, and other northwest wildlife. Then, you'll pull into Friday Harbor, where you'll have two hours to explore shops, visit a museum, have a friendly conversation, and enjoy lunch. Afterwards, you'll board your boat again and head back to Port Townsend, but not before making a stop at Smith Island, where you're sure to see Steller and California sea lions basking in the sun. Your day of adventure winds up as you dock again in Port Townsend at 5:00 p.m.

- Adults: $115.00 – Children (2-10): $85 – Infants: Free
- Bicycle / Kayak: $15
- Call prior to your arrival to check dates available for your trip and to receive additional details.
- Arrive 45 minutes prior to your departure. Note that boarding closes 15 minutes prior to departure. *Due to stringent departure requirements, late arrivals will be cancelled with no refunds.*

For more information about Puget Sound Express and these whale watching trips, visit: www.PugetSoundExpress.com

Puget Sound Express
227 Jackson Street
Port Townsend, WA 98368
360-385-5288

Directions and Parking:

Per Puget Sound Express: *Our free parking lot is 2.5 blocks **straight** past our office. As you approach our office on Jackson Street, passengers may wish to get out at the office and check in while the driver parks the vehicle. To reach the parking lot, proceed past the office on Jackson Street to the **STOP** sign. **Go straight** across the road and proceed 2.5 blocks **until you reach pavement again**. Look for the Puget Sound Express parking sign on your right.*

www.Discover-Washington.com

☐ **Chetzemoka Park**

Located seven blocks northwest of Water Street, on the top of a hill at the north end of the Uptown neighborhood, is 6-acre Chetzemoka Park. Named after Chief Chetzemoka, the park is a beautiful spot of solitude high on a bluff overlooking Admiralty Inlet, Puget Sound, and the Cascade Mountains far in the distance.

Chetzemoka Park
1000 Jackson Street
Port Townsend, WA 98368
360-385-2700

- Open Daily – 5:00 a.m. to Sunset

PORT TOWNSEND - OUTLYING ATTRACTIONS

 ☐ **Alpenfire Cider**

Either as a side trip while in Port Townsend or a convenient stop on your way out to Sequim...provided you're running a bit late on a weekend morning...we highly recommend a stop at Alpenfire Cider. Here, "Bear" and Nancy Bishop artfully craft the finest

of ciders from the over 1,000 apple trees in their orchard. Grown organically and pesticide free, these trees produce the rare cider apples used for centuries in the cider regions of Europe, and when blended with heirloom apples grown locally, produce small vintages in a variety of award-winning styles and flavors that "range from old world to new world." Stop in for a taste, visit with Bear and Nancy, wander through the orchard, and pick up a gift bottle for family and friends.

    Alpenfire Cider
    220 Pocket Lane
    Port Townsend, WA 98368   (360-379-8915)

- Open: March through October – Saturdays and Sundays – 12:00 p.m. to 5:00 p.m.

 Port Townsend Wheel-In Motor Movie – Drive-In Theatre

After your day is done, plan to enjoy a first-run movie in a last-of-its-kind theatre...The Port Townsend Wheel-In Motor Movie. Pull up in your car, hook the classic drive-in speaker on your window, and enjoy a blast to the past as the silver screen illuminates the night air with adventure, romance, mystery, or comedy.

The Port Townsend Wheel-In Motor Movie opens in April and is located a little south of Port Townsend. Check what's playing by visiting www.PTWheelinMotorMovie.com

    Port Townsend Wheel-In Motor Movie
    210 Theatre Road
    Port Townsend, WA 98368   (360-385-0859)

Note that the Port Townsend Wheel-In Motor Movie's snack bar serves pizza, hamburgers, hot dogs, nachos, soft drinks, and more.

SEASONAL EVENTS

 ☐ **Port Townsend Farmers Market**

Enjoy a Saturday morning or early afternoon perusing the local wares of the Port Townsend Farmers Market. Pick up some fresh fruits and vegetables, cut flowers, artisan pastries and baked goods, live plants, handcrafted artwork, LaughinGnome pottery, and more while listening to local live music. The market opens the first Saturday in April and runs through late December.

> Port Townsend Farmers Market
> 650 Tyler Street - Tyler Street between Lawrence and Clay
> Port Townsend, WA 98368
>
> - Open:
>
>   - Early April to Oct. - Saturdays 9:00 a.m. to 2:00 p.m.
>   - November to late December - 10:00 a.m. to 2:00 p.m.

 ☐ **Port Townsend Art Walk**

Explore, discover, and enjoy the artwork of local artists on the first Saturday of every month during the Port Townsend Art Walk. Stroll through the old town area and stop in at art galleries, boutiques, restaurants, even real estate offices to have a glass of wine, meet a new friend, and find a piece of art that captures your imagination.

When: First Saturday of every month - 5:30 p.m. to 8:00 p.m.

 ☐ **Port Townsend Wooden Boat Festival**

In early September of every year, thousands of mariners and landlubbers alike from near and far walk, drive, ferry, and sail to Port Townsend to experience the Wooden Boat Festival, a festive event showcasing over 300 beautiful wooden boats large and small which reflect the fine craftsmanship and traditions of wooden boatbuilding. Hosted by the Northwest Maritime Center and occurring over an entire weekend, the festival offers visitors the opportunity to get their sea legs as they speak with boat owners, board and inspect boats, join a rowboat ride in the harbor, sail aboard a schooner, and enjoy dozens of educational presentations at the center and nearby marina. In addition, walk through downtown Port Townsend while enjoying live music, great food, fun kids' activities, artwork, visiting with local artists, and much more all day long.

Tickets:

- One-Day: $20
- Multi-Day – Friday – Sunday: $40
- Note that discounts are available for Seniors, Students 13 – 18, and active military personnel. Kids 12 and under are admitted at no charge.

For additional information, including this year's festival dates, visit www.NWMaritime.org. Please note that dogs are not allowed at the festival.

Wooden Boat Festival
Northwest Maritime Center
431 Water Street
Port Townsend, WA 98368

 **Port Townsend Film Festival**

The Port Townsend Film Festival is a *reely* big deal. The science, art and passion of moviemaking are showcased over 4 days during the third weekend in September every year as eight different theatres in the historic downtown district present feature narratives, documentary shorts, major motion pictures, silent movies, interviews with filmmakers, special dinners, and much more, all beginning at 9:00 a.m. Friday morning. You'll even have an opportunity to watch family-oriented movies outside each evening during the festival while sitting atop hay bales in the street! (You can also bring your own lawn chairs.)

Learn about this year's films, the festival schedule, pricing for passes, "How to Fest", and more by visiting www.PTFilmFest.com

www.Discover-Washington.com

NOTES

www.Discover-Washington.com

Alexander's Castle - Fort Worden

Fort Worden at Port Townsend

Fort Worden

Located 2 miles north of Port Townsend is Fort Worden State Park. Established over 100 years ago as a military installation, it housed nearly 1,000 troops and officers who manned 41 artillery pieces placed high atop the bluffs of Artillery Hill as part of the "Triangle of Fire" designed to protect Puget Sound, Admiralty Inlet and the Strait of Juan de Fuca from attack by enemy vessels.

Today, Fort Worden is a tranquil 432 acre state park welcoming visitors to explore its trails, visit its museums, walk its beaches, venture out to the Point Wilson lighthouse, and even stay the night in one of the fort's 100 different historical buildings, cottages and large Victorian-era Officers' homes.

Note that a Washington State Discover Pass is required when visiting the trails or beaches of the park, *but not the buildings or sites within the main campus area.* The park is equipped with an automated pay station where visitors may purchase either a one day or annual pass.

Guests staying in one of the 36 different overnight accommodations at Fort Worden, or at any of the campgrounds within the park, may use the parking pass issued when checking in as a "complimentary" Discover Pass during their stay. If you wish to visit Artillery Hill or the beaches *before* you check in and receive your pass, then you may either purchase a day pass or simply park somewhere within the main campus and walk to your destination.

www.Discover-Washington.com

 **Hike Atop Artillery Hill**

Start your exploration of Fort Worden with a hike up to the batteries atop Artillery Hill. Walk through the bunkers, pill boxes, ammunition depots, and observation platforms, which are all formed out of concrete, and try to imagine the massive "disappearing guns", as well as the hundreds of troops, that used to stand on watch here as they protected the vast open seas below. Plan on spending some time to sit and enjoy the view from atop the batteries or at different spots as you hike along the Bluff Trail. You'll find the best views at the northern batteries. Excellent maps for the trails of Artillery Hill and all of Fort Worden are available at the Commons building, Artillery Museum Gift Shop, and elsewhere. In addition, you'll find detailed trail descriptions at www.FWFriends.org

Note: There are some large drop offs within the battery structures, many without any form of protective railings, so you'll want to keep small children close at hand.

 **Picnic Lunch Atop Artillery Hill?**

As you make your way about today, consider returning to Artillery Hill to enjoy a picnic lunch while enjoying the view.

www.Discover-Washington.com

 Point Wilson Lighthouse

Built in 1913, and featuring a fourth-order Fresnel lens from the original 1879 lighthouse located here, the Point Wilson Lighthouse today serves as an important navigational tool for ships large and small navigating the entrance to Admiralty Inlet.

Walk or drive to the parking area near the lighthouse and then make your way a short distance to both the lighthouse and the lighthouse keeper's home. Note that both structures are unmanned and not open to the public.

> Point Wilson Light House
> 200 Battery Way
> Port Townsend, WA 98368

 Puget Sound Coast Artillery Museum

Learn all about Fort Worden and its role as a military installation charged with protecting Puget Sound, Admiralty Inlet, and the Strait of Juan de Fuca beginning in the late 1800s and continuing through the mid-1950s. Numerous exhibits, displays, videos, and military items explain all about the fort, its history, and the daily lives of the soldiers and officers who lived and served here. During the summer months, from Memorial Day Weekend through Labor Day, museum volunteers provide guided tours of the fortifications each Saturday.

Admission:

- Adults: $4.00
- Children (6-12): $2.00
- Children 5 and Under: Free
- Immediate Family (2 Generations): $10.00
- Active Duty Service Members: Free

Puget Sound Coast Artillery Museum
Building #201
200 Battery Way
Port Townsend, WA 98368
360-385-0373

- Open: Daily – 11:00 a.m. to 4:00 p.m.

 Commanding Officers Quarters Museum

One of Fort Worden's finest buildings, the 1904 Commanding Officers Quarters is a nearly 6,000 square foot Victorian-era home operated today as a museum depicting the lifestyles of Fort Worden's commanding officers. Admire the detailed architecture of the building's exterior before stepping inside to see interpretive displays and items from daily life at the turn of the prior century in this impressively curated and finely restored home.

Note that the Commanding Officers Quarters, combined with the Rothschild House Museum and Jefferson Art & History Museum, make up a trio of museums in Port Townsend that are covered by a single discounted pass, which is available for purchase here. The following rates are for the Commanding Officers Quarters only:

Admission:

- Adults: $6.00, Seniors $5.00
- Children (3-12): $1.00 (Children 3 and Under: Free)
- Active Duty Service Members & Family: Free

 Port Townsend Marine Science Center

The Port Townsend Marine Science Center consists of two buildings; an aquarium out on a pier, and the other a building nearby on land, which tells the story of an orca named Hope.

Aquarium (On the Pier)

Interactive displays reveal the life of fish and invertebrates living just off shore in the Salish Sea. Reach into a "touch tank" of sea anemones, sea urchins and star fish, visit with a Giant Pacific Octopus, view tiny plankton up close through a microscope, and if you time it right on a Saturday afternoon during the summer, you just may be able to help with a feeding or two.

Museum (On Shore – Opposite the Aquarium)

In 2002, the body of a grown female orca was found washed up on shore near Port Townsend. She had died as a result of having one of the highest levels of toxic chemicals ever recorded in a marine mammal. Step inside the museum to learn about "Hope", the orca, and through interactive displays discover how the environment in the Salish Sea impacts us all.

Admission:

- Adults: $7.00
- Youth: (6-17) $5.00
- Children (5 and Under): Free
- Winter months – December through March: Admission by donation.

Port Townsend Marine Science Center
532 Battery Way
Port Townsend, WA 98368
360-385-5582

Open:

- Spring: (Through the end of March) Friday through Sunday – 12:00 p.m. to 5:00 p.m.

- Summer: (Memorial Day through Labor Day) Wednesday through Monday – 11:00 a.m. to 5:00 p.m.

- Fall: (Beginning early September) Friday through Sunday – 12:00 p.m. to 5:00 p.m.

- Winter: (Beginning early December) Friday through Sunday – 12:00 p.m. to 5:00 p.m. Note that during the winter, the museum is open, but the aquarium is closed.

www.Discover-Washington.com

 **Kayak Tours & Rentals**

Want to add a fun and exciting aspect to your visit to Fort Worden? Then rent a kayak and experience life out on the open water!

Port Townsend PaddleSports offers visitors both tours and rentals, and beginners are more than welcome.

Tours

Scheduled every Saturday and Sunday during July and August, guided tours with a skilled and knowledgeable guide are the perfect way to experience and explore the waters in the Fort Worden and Port Townsend area. Plan to arrive 15 to 30 minutes prior to the tour departure time to register, become familiar with the kayaks, and be fitted for life vests.

Fort Worden Tour - 2 Hours

Learn all about the marine life in and above the waters off Fort Worden from a knowledgeable guide, all while keeping an eye out for harbor seals, river otters, bald eagles, tufted puffins, and even porpoises and orcas.

The Fort Worden Tour is perfect for first-timers, families, and those with limited time in their schedule. Meet at 9:00 a.m. for a 9:30 a.m. departure at the kayak station opposite the Port Townsend Marine Science Center dock at Fort Worden. This tour occurs at 9:30 a.m. every Sunday in July and August.

Rates: Adults: $50 – Children: (8 – 12 Years) $39 - Minimum 3 paddlers. Private tours for couples are also available, and you can pick the date and time of your departure.

Downtown Tour – 3 Hours

Leaving from the same beach used for the Fort Worden kayak tour at Fort Worden, you'll paddle south before heading starboard (right) around Port Hudson. You'll then continue south along the Port Townsend waterfront where you'll explore this Victorian seaport from the water instead of from land. Before you begin making your way back, you'll come ashore at the Northwest Maritime Center to stop in at Velocity Coffee, where you can reward your adventurous spirit with a hot drink and fresh-baked pastry.

Beginners are more than welcome on this tour. Meet at 9:00 a.m. for a 9:30 a.m. departure at the kayak station opposite the Port Townsend Marine Science Center dock at Fort Worden. This tour occurs at 9:30 a.m. on most Saturdays during July and August.

Rates: Adults: $65 – Children: (8 – 12 Years) $45 – Minimum 3 paddlers. Private tours for couples are also available, and you can pick the date and time of your departure.

Kayak and Paddleboard Rentals

Want to set out on your own? Then rent a kayak or paddleboard and hit the high seas! Single and double kayak and paddleboard rentals are available, and no experience is necessary. Port Townsend PaddleSports will provide you with a short lesson and helpful hints, as well as inform you as to which areas to explore and which to avoid.

Note that the waters of Puget Sound, Admiralty Inlet, and the Salish Sea are inland from the Pacific Ocean, and as such are affected by tides and strong currents, as well as wind. It is recommended that you enjoy kayaking in the morning, when waters are the calmest, the lighting is nice, and the birds are more active. That said, the areas close to shore that Port Townsend PaddleSports recommends are usually calm and easy to navigate.

Because you are out on the open water, be sure to wear a hat, sunglasses, and sunscreen, and bring a full water bottle. Visit the FAQ section at www.PTPaddleSports.com/faq to learn more.

Port Townsend PaddleSports
Fort Worden State Park
100 Harbor Defense Way
Port Townsend, WA 98368
360-379-3608

www.Discover-Washington.com

NOTES

www.Discover-Washington.com

New Dungeness Light Station

Sequim

Sequim

Located approximately half way between Port Townsend and Port Angeles, the charming town of Sequim welcomes visitors with an abundance of outdoor activities, cultural events, annual festivals, and more. Hike the Dungeness Spit out to the New Dungeness Lighthouse, experience the animal kingdom up close at the Olympic Game Farm, take a flight in a colorful hot air balloon, see an abundance of lavender fields in bloom, or set out to explore the Olympic Discovery Trail. This and much more await you in Sequim!

 **Lunch at Fat Smitty's?**

When you reach the junction of Hwy 20 and Hwy 101 on the way to Sequim, you'll find Fat Smitty's restaurant. That big hamburger you see outside? That's the Fat Smitty Burger, and the real one is only a tad smaller. If you're feeling hungry, stop inside for a bite. Order the Fat Smitty Burger and ask to have it split in two. You'll pay $1.00 extra, but they'll bring you two plates, two portions of fries or onion rings, and one half each of a Fat Smitty Burger, which is really a whole burger. While you're dining, take a look at the tens of thousands of dollar bills that have been tacked to the walls and ceiling of the restaurant.

Note that Fat Smitty's offers a variety of items on their menu besides burgers. *Be sure to bring cash, as that is all they accept.* An ATM is located on site, however.

Fat Smitty's
282624 US-101
Port Townsend, WA 98368
360-385-4099

- Open: Daily – 10:30 a.m. to 7:00 p.m.

 ## Sequim Visitor Center

Stop in at the Sequim Visitor Center, conveniently located on the way into town, and visit with the friendly staff who are more than happy to tell you all about the area, its history, and its many attractions. You'll also find an excellent map of Sequim here.

Sequim Visitor Center
1192 East Washington Street
Sequim, WA 98382
360-683-6690

- Open: Monday through Saturday – 10:00 a.m. to 4:00 p.m., Sunday – 10:00 a.m. to 1:00 p.m.

 ## 1945 Grain Elevator

Perhaps oddly juxtaposed as it sits within a small strip mall, the towering old Clallam Co-op granary provides a nod back to the 1940s, when it was built as a grain elevator to serve local farmers in the area. Today, it holds a popular Mexican restaurant and a cellular tower.

Sequim Grain Elevator
531 West Washington Street
Sequim, WA 98382

 ## Museum & Arts Center

Stop by for a visit and to learn about the natural and cultural history of Sequim and the surrounding region in this new and well-curated museum. See a beautifully restored 1907 REO Model B Roundabout, which is reportedly the first automobile ever driven in the Dungeness Valley, the partial skull and bones of a 100,000 year-old Columbian mammoth, the handcrafted racing boat that won a gold medal in the 1936 Olympics in Germany, and a collection of fascinating artifacts and exhibits reflecting the daily lives of Sequim's early and more modern day inhabitants.

Museum & Arts Center
544 North Sequim Ave.
Sequim, WA 98382
360-681-2257

- Open: Tuesday through Saturday – 11:00 a.m. to 4:00 p.m. Also 5:00 p.m. to 8:00 p.m. during "First Friday Art Walks"

www.Discover-Washington.com

 **Olympic Game Farm**

The Olympic Peninsula is a world filled with fascinating animals. Orcas and humpback whales swim in the deep cool waters of the Salish Sea, while deer and elk walk the forests and high ridges of Olympic National Park. At the Olympic Game Park, however, animals of a different sort greet you as you drive your car through this wildlife exhibit. Bison, llamas, Sika deer, peacocks, yaks and more approach your car in anticipation of being fed a slice from the loaf of wheat bread you purchased at the entrance. Behind fences and cages, lions, tigers, foxes, bears, zebras and other exotic animals look on as you pass.

During the summer months, you'll find a petting zoo and freshwater aquarium available, as well. In addition, majestic bald eagles perch in the trees during the winter and spring months as they watch the action unfold below.

Admission:

>   Adults (15+): $17.00
>   Children (6-14): $14.00
>   Seniors (55+): $14.00
>   Olympic Game Farm
>   1423 Ward Road
>   Sequim, WA 98382
>   360-683-4295

- Open: Daily – 9:00 a.m. to 5:00 p.m. (Sat: 6:00 p.m.)

Note: *For proper visitor safety, convertibles and jeeps are required to have tops up and side panels on at all times.*

 ## Port Williams / Marlyn Nelson County Park

Marlyn Nelson County Park is named after Sequim resident Marlyn Wayne Nelson, who died at the age of 19 from injuries sustained in the attack at Pearl Harbor while aboard the USS California. Visit the small shoreline park to pay your respects to Mr. Nelson, take in the view of the Cascade Mountains across Puget Sound, stroll its pebbly beach, and enjoy a picnic in the afternoon sun.

Port Williams / Marlyn Nelson County Park
2499 Port Williams Road
Sequim, WA 98383
360-417-2291

 ## Manis Mastodon Site

On August 8, 1977, Farmer Emanuel Manis was digging on his property when he suddenly discovered an amazing find...two large tusks of an American mastodon. Further archaeological excavation revealed a rib bone, as well as a fragmented skull and the remains of caribou, bison, and even spear points dating back more than 10,000 years. Visit this two-acre site on the U.S. National Register of Historic Places to learn more about the ancient history of the Northern Olympic Peninsula, as well as the animals that roamed here. You'll find the Manis Mastodon Site approximately 1,000 feet south of the Happy Valley Alpaca Ranch, just off Lester Way.
Photo courtesy of the Peninsula Daily News

 ## Happy Valley Alpaca Ranch

Located across the field from Molten Momma's Hot Shop is the Happy Valley Alpaca Ranch. Stop in to meet the alpacas, take a tour of the ranch, see some baby alpacas in the springtime, and find a handmade treasure in the gift shop, which offers hats, mittens, shawls, jackets, blankets, and much more.

Schedule a time to tour the ranch and learn about the world of alpacas, their long history in their native lands of South America, and their soft luxurious fur that is prized for its warmth and durability. Tours of the ranch are available at a time that is convenient for you during weekdays and Saturdays. To make a reservation, call 360-681-0948.

Happy Valley Alpaca Ranch
4629 Happy Valley Road
Sequim, WA 98382
360-681-0948

- Open: Saturday – 10:00 a.m. to 2:00 p.m.

www.Discover-Washington.com

Railroad Bridge Park – Dungeness River Audubon Center

In 1915, the Chicago, Milwaukee and St. Paul Railroad owned the railway that spanned across the North Olympic Peninsula from Port Townsend to west of Lake Crescent. Long ago abandoned, today this rail line is part of the Olympic Discovery Trail, an amazing multi-use non-motorized path that spans all the way from Port Townsend west to La Push, on the Pacific Ocean.

Travelers along the Olympic Discovery Trail will come upon the 28-acre Railroad Bridge Park, which is home to both the Dungeness River Audubon Center and a large railway bridge.

The Dungeness River Audubon Center is a non-profit educational and interpretive center run in conjunction with the Jamestown S'Klallam Tribe, offering inspiring experiences for visitors of all ages, as it showcases the birds, fish, amphibians and other animals of the Olympic Peninsula and Pacific Northwest.

In addition, nearby stands an impressive 1915 railway bridge that is one of the last, if not *the* last, remaining Howe truss bridges in the Northwest. Built to carry lumber trains across the Dungeness River in the early 1900s, today it carries hikers, cyclists, and other non-motorized travelers as part of the Olympic Discovery Trail.

Drive to the park, park your car, and walk a short distance to either the Audubon Center or the bridge.

Railroad Bridge Park / Dungeness River Audubon Center
2151 West Hendrickson Road
Sequim, WA 98382
360-681-4076

Open:

- April through October - Tuesday through Saturday - 10:00 a.m. to 4:00 p.m., Sunday - 12:00 p.m. to 4:00 p.m.

- November through March - Tuesday through Friday - 10:00 a.m. to 4:00 p.m., Saturday - 12:00 p.m. to 4:00 p.m.

 ## Olympic Discovery Trail

As you travel across the northern Olympic Peninsula, you'll periodically cross paths with the *Olympic Discovery Trail - The Pathway to the Pacific*. At over 130 miles long, it traverses the width of the Olympic Peninsula from Port Townsend all the way to La Push on the Pacific Coast. Closed to motorized traffic, the trail takes bikers, hikers, walkers and more through a collection of towns, cool forests, tunnels and open fields, as well as along high bluffs, pristine lakes, and rushing white water streams, all with breath-taking ocean and mountain views.

Currently, the entire length of the trail is yet to be completed, but considerable work is being done every year by a large group of stakeholders and volunteers with the expectation for the trail to be fully completed by 2030. By then, all of the trestles will be finished, (There are

three that are over 400' long) all bridges will be in place, land acquisitions and right of-ways negotiated, and smooth paving for the entire route laid down. This is truly a world-class cycling/hiking/walking destination that you will want to make plans to visit and enjoy once it is finished. Abundant trail heads, rest stops, picnic areas, campgrounds and local bike-friendly attractions dot the trail, making it perfect for a unique multi-day adventure.

Historic Dungeness Schoolhouse

Standing as a stately reminder of times past in Sequim is the Historic Dungeness Schoolhouse. Built in 1892, complete with its distinctive belfry and fine architectural details, it is a nod back to the time when students of all ages and grades attended classes here in only two classrooms on the first floor, while the teacher lived on the second.

Today, the school is owned by the Sequim Museum & Arts Center and is used periodically for community events. In addition, one of the two classrooms has been preserved as a historic schoolroom exhibit, appearing today just as it did on the first day of school in 1892. Visitors may visit the classroom by appointment only, which may be made by contacting the Sequim Museum & Arts Center at 360-681-2257, or by emailing your request to SequimMuseum@Olypen.com. Advance notice of 24 hours is appreciated, but not always mandatory. Tours are free, but donations are gladly accepted.

Historic Dungeness Schoolhouse
2781 Towne Road
Sequim, WA 98382

Dungeness Spit / New Dungeness Light Station / Dungeness National Wildlife Refuge

Situated north of Sequim is Dungeness Spit, the longest natural sand spit in the United States. Stretching far out into the Strait of Juan de Fuca, this narrow strip of land is anchored on the shore end by the Dungeness Wildlife Refuge, and at its far end, the New Dungeness Light Station. We recommend you enjoy the short paved hike through the Dungeness Wildlife Refuge to the two viewing platforms overlooking Dungeness Spit before dropping down to the spit itself for a short hike. It is unlikely that you will have time to hike all the way out to the lighthouse and back, as the trail is a total of 10 miles round-trip (5 Hours) *and should be hiked only at low tide.*

Both the Dungeness National Wildlife Refuge and Dungeness Spit are open 365 days a year, from 9:00 a.m. to 5:00 p.m. Note that there is a $3.00 Daily Use Fee for visiting the refuge and the spit, and this is paid at the parking area / trailhead.

Dungeness National Wildlife Refuge

In 1915, President Woodrow Wilson established the Dungeness National Wildlife Refuge as a sanctuary for migratory and native birds. Here, the narrow Dungeness Spit provides protection with its quiet bay, nutrient-rich tideflats, a safe sandy beach for harbor seals and their pups, and abundant eelgrass for the rearing of young salmon and steelhead.

You'll walk through the forested portion of the 772-acre refuge when you begin your hike to Dungeness Spit from the parking area. Prior to dropping down to the spit, you'll find two viewing platforms, both of which allow you to look out over the spit and bay portion of the refuge. Telescopes are provided here.

New Dungeness Light Station

At the northern end of the Dungeness Spit is the New Dungeness Light Station. Built in 1857 it was the first lighthouse ever established in the Washington Territory.

Nearby stands the Lighthouse Keeper's House and museum. Beautifully restored and maintained, it hosts volunteers who spend one week at a time during the summer months living at the house and performing the duties of a lighthouse keeper, including welcoming visitors, offering tours, shining the brass, and even mowing the lawn.

Tours of the lighthouse and museum are available seven days a week from 9:00 a.m. to 5:00 p.m. for those who hike the 10 miles round-trip to the lighthouse during low tide, a trek that is made annually by many locals. In addition to learning about the lighthouse, Dungeness Spit, and the Native Americans who once lived here, visitors may climb stairs to the top of the lighthouse for a captivating view of the Strait of Juan de Fuca, as well as Canada in the distance. *Photo © Kraig Anderson - LighthouseFriends.com*

New Dungeness Light Station
Dungeness Spit
Sequim, WA 98382

- Open: Daily – 9:00 a.m. to 5:00 p.m.

- Public restrooms and water are available at the lighthouse, but that is all. No food or other supplies are available here.

Hiking Out to the Lighthouse

Visitors may reach the lighthouse by hiking 5 miles (10 miles round-trip) along Dungeness Spit to its northern end. Note that you'll want to make this hike, both out and back, during low tide when you can more easily hike on the sandy beach at the shoreline.

Begin the hike at the same parking area and trailhead used for the Dungeness National Wildlife Refuge, as described on page 86. From the viewing platforms, drop down the short trail to the spit and begin your hike.

There are no fees required to visit the lighthouse, but donations are greatly appreciated for its ongoing maintenance in the harsh marine environment.

Tips for a Safe Hike

- *Check the Tide Table in advance at the trailhead kiosk before you start. Attempt the hike only at low tide, which allows you to hike along the sandy beach.* High tides require you to climb over driftwood logs and can add several hours to our trip. The spit is rarely breached by storms, but when it does happen the lighthouse becomes an island until the next low tide.

- Allow 5 hours for the round trip and a rest at the lighthouse.

- Refer to the Refuge Map for designated hiking areas. Walking is allowed only along the north side of the spit, below the boundary markers. There is no public access on the south side of the spit or the area past the lighthouse.

- Check the weather before beginning your hike. There is no shelter until you reach the lighthouse. Sunscreen should always be worn during the spring, summer and fall months.

- You must be out of the refuge by sunset, which is posted daily at the entrance. Be sure to bring a flashlight or headlamp with you.

- There is no transport back other than on foot. Footwear suitable for hiking on sand and rocks or climbing over logs is recommended.

- *There is a drinking fountain located at the lighthouse, but there is no food or drink available here. Bring extra food and water, as this is a 10 mile hike.*

- Because you are hiking in a National Wildlife Refuge, dogs are not allowed.

- Of course, the very best way to visit the lighthouse is to get a ride out as part of the Keeper Program! Learn more about this unique volunteer opportunity at www.NewDungenessLighthouse.com/keeper-program

Directions:

From Sequim: Travel west on Lotzgesell Road to Voice of America Road W, which is on your right 0.2 miles before reaching Kitchen-Dick Road. Turn north onto Voice of America Road W and follow this through the refuge to the parking area and trailhead at the end of the road.

From Hwy 101: Turn north onto Kitchen-Dick Road and follow this a little over 3 miles to where it curves east into Lotzgesell Road. Look for the signed entrance to the Dungeness Spit on your left in 0.2 mile.

Note that there is a $3.00 Daily Use Fee for visiting the refuge and the spit, and this is paid at the parking area / trailhead.

 ## Agnew Grocery and Feed

Everyone within 100 miles knows of Agnew Grocery and Feed, and you should too! This small mom and pop store has welcomed customers since 1926, and we're sure it looks much the same today as it did back then. Step inside to say "Hello", grab a snack and drink for the road, and then make your way out back to meet a collection of small friendly farm animals, including pigs, goats, turkeys, peacocks, and more.

Agnew Grocery and Feed
2863 Old Olympic Highway
Port Angeles, WA 98362
360-452-2466

- Open: Monday through Saturday – 7:00 a.m. to 8:00 p.m., Sunday – 7:00 a.m. to 6:00 p.m.

www.Discover-Washington.com

 ## Sequim Roosevelt Elk Herd

They may be very elusive, but they are impressive. The Olympic Peninsula is home to a few different herds of Roosevelt Elk, one of which often resides in the Sequim area. Consisting of about 25 to 40 animals, the Sequim herd tends to favor the fields north and south of Hwy 101 as you begin to approach town. If you see caution lights flashing on the highway, that is an indicator that the herd is in the area and you should drive with caution.

View with Caution

While they may appear to be docile, Roosevelt Elk are wild animals prone to agitation, and as such they should be viewed with caution from a distance and never approached. Weighing up to 1,000 lbs., they are very fast and agile. Given the choice, they will avoid humans, but will become aggressive if people get too close, approach their young calves, or block their path of escape.

 ## Lavender Capital of North America

With a sunny and drier climate similar to that found in the south of France, Sequim is one of the best places in North America to grow lavender. A prolific herb that blooms primarily in July, it fills fields in the area with long rows and rows of bright purple blossoms that are stunning to see and amazing to walk among. Honey bees, bumble bees, butterflies and more flock to its fragrant bright flowers and make for the perfect photo capturing the essence of summer.

As you travel around Sequim during the summer months, you'll find many lavender farms offering flowers for the picking, plus an abundance of natural lavender related items for sale, including soaps, essential oils, scents, candles, and more. Note that many of these farms are also open year-round.

Sequim Lavender Festival/Weekend

During the third weekend in July, when field after field of brightly colored purple lavender blossoms are at their peak, Sequim bustles with activity as it hosts the popular Sequim Lavender Festival. Twelve small family-owned lavender farms welcome visitors from all across the northwest and the country during this festive 3-day celebration showcasing the over 110,000 lavender plants that grow in the area.

Learn more at www.LavenderFestival.com, and be sure to stop in at the Sequim Visitor Center (Page 78) to learn about the festival and to get a map to the 12 participating farms.

Note: Some of the locals will tell you to visit on the weekends immediately before and after the Sequim Lavender Festival if you'd like fewer crowds and the opportunity to move at a slower pace while visiting with the farmers. You'll miss out on the vendors, live music, local food and products, however.

Take Flight in a Hot Air Balloon

Jump ...or float... at this chance to take a scenic flight in a hot air balloon high over Sequim. Drift quietly through the air as you take in stunning views of the Olympic Mountains, the Strait of Juan de Fuca, the entire Sequim-Dungeness

Valley, and even Canada from your lofty perch suspended under a colorful hot air balloon.

- Flights are about 1 hour.
- The basket holds up to 4 people / 700 lbs.
- $300 Per person – Children are $2 per pound.
- You must have a reservation to fly, so please call at least 2 to 3 days in advance to make your flight reservation. Note that last-minute openings are sometimes available.
- Flights are available throughout the year, weather permitting.
- Prior to your flight, you'll receive paperwork that describes what to expect, what to wear, what not to wear, waiver information, directions, etc.
- Hot air ballooning is very weather dependent. Rain, wind, fog, and low cloud cover may cancel your flight. Call at least 2 days prior to your scheduled flight time to check the status of your flight.

Morning Star Balloon Company
Sequim Valley Airport
468 Dorothy Hunt Lane
Sequim, WA 98382
360-601-2433

- Open: Daily – 6:30 a.m. to 9:30 a.m. (3 Hours in the morning)

www.Discover-Washington.com

 ☐ **Wing Walking on a Biplane**

This is truly a unique thrill-seeking adventure of a lifetime!

Taking a full day, you'll arrive early in the morning and spend 4 to 5 hours learning about the world of wing walking and practicing the movements and skills necessary to climb onto the upper wing of a bright red 1943 Boeing Stearman biplane while wearing a safety harness and cable. Once you have committed every move and hold to muscle memory, and fully learned about every safety precaution, you'll take to the skies. High above the Sequim Valley, the pilot will then power back to a slow glide and give you the go ahead to climb out of the cockpit and make your way to the upper wing, where you'll securely strap yourself in. Soon, you're barnstorming above Sequim as the biplane perform loops, rolls, and hammerheads while you have the best seat in the house...and one of the biggest thrills of your lifetime!

- No wing walking experience is required.
- *This experience involves a full day beginning about 9:00 a.m., so you'll want to add one day to your road trip.*
- Reservations should be made 2 to 3 months in advance, though last-minute openings sometimes occur.
- Longer courses are available, including a two-day course offering twice as much flying.
- Flights are offered spring through fall, though the best months are during July, August, and September.
- Learn more at www.MasonWingwalking.com
- Note that the Mason Wing Walking Academy is located near the entrance to the Dungeness Wildlife Refuge.
- Open: Spring through Fall

- Cost:
    - $985 One person, full course, upper and lower wing.
    - $650 One person, introductory course, upper wing.
    - $1,800 Two-day course. Spread your training over two days and fly twice as much.
    - Discounts are available for multiple fliers

Mason Wing Walking Academy
61 Greywolf Air Ct.
Sequim, WA 98382
360-775-1213

 **Sequim Farmers Market**

Stop by to see a bounty of locally grown and handcrafted products by farmers, craftsmen, and artisans. Peruse handmade greeting cards, clothing, jewelry, and gifts for man's best friend, as well as fresh fruits, vegetables, raw honey, spices, lavender products, baked goods, and much more, all with vendors offering delicious food, pleasant conversation, and live music.

Located in downtown Sequim on the Civic Center Plaza, at the corner of Cedar Street and Sequim Avenue

- Open: May to October – 9:00 a.m. to 3:00 p.m.

www.Discover-Washington.com

 **Sequim Irrigation Festival**

Every year, during the first two weekends of May, the entire community of Sequim and the surrounding area come together during the Sequim Irrigation Festival to celebrate the tireless work of D. R. "Crazy" Callen and his crew who, in 1896, brought water from the Dungeness River to the dry prairies of Sequim. In what is the oldest continuing festival in Washington, residents, guests, and visitors alike gather to enjoy a variety of festive community events, including the Crazy Daze Breakfast, First Friday Art Walk, the crowning of the queen and her court, an exciting carnival, explosive fireworks, and of course, a grand parade with colorful elaborate floats!

www.Discover-Washington.com

NOTES

www.Discover-Washington.com

The Kalakala - World's First Streamlined Vessel

PORT ANGELES

Port Angeles

Situated on the northern shoreline of the Olympic Peninsula, Port Angeles serves as a gateway to numerous lands and adventures. The Black Ball Ferry departs here for Victoria, B.C., Canada, where travelers enjoy an abundance of attractions. Tour operators launch into the Strait of Juan de Fuca to marvel at gray whales, orcas, and humpbacks, while modern day explorers journey south to the majestic alpine peaks of Olympic National Park, and intrepid travelers set out west to discover the rugged history and captivating beauty of coastal lands beyond.

☐ Port Angeles Information Center

Stop by the Port Angeles Information Center to learn more about Port Angeles, the surrounding region, and the Olympic Peninsula, as well as the many events that happen in the area throughout the year. The staff is very helpful and more than happy to answer any questions you may have.

Port Angeles Regional Chamber of Commerce
121 East Railroad Avenue
Port Angeles, WA 98363
360-452-2363

- Open: Monday through Friday – 10:00 a.m. to 5:00 p.m., Saturday – 10:00 a.m. to 4:00 p.m., and Sunday – 11:00 a.m. to 2:00 p.m.

Note that the Port Angeles Underground Heritage Tour meets and begins its tours here.

 ## ☐ Island Adventures Whale Watching

The waters just off of Port Angeles are recognized as being one of the finest whale watching destinations in the country. Here, humpback whales are making a comeback with hundreds visiting these waters every summer. In addition, countless gray whales move through the Salish Sea during their yearly migration to and from Alaska, while pods of orcas hunt in the deep cool waters in search of salmon and other prey.

Join Island Adventures Whale Watching as they set out aboard the Island Explorer in search of whales and other fascinating sea life. Your tour may take you into the Strait of Juan de Fuca, east toward the beautiful San Juan Islands, or north to the Race Rock Ecological Preserve in Canada, where you're guaranteed to experience the breath-taking and often emotional thrill of spotting these magnificent marine mammals.

Tours occur during May through October and last between four to five hours.

- Late May – Mid-June
  Adults: $99 – Discounted Adults: $89

- Mid-June – Early September
  Adults: $109 – Discounted Adults: $99

- Early September through October
  Adults: $99 – Discounted Adults: $89

- Children (Ages 3 – 17): $69

- Children under 3: $1

Note: You can save $20 to $30 when you book your whale watching tour 30 days in advance via their web site. www.Island-Adventures.com

Island Adventures Whale Watching
115 East Railroad Avenue
Port Angeles, WA 98362
360-293-4215

To check in for your tour, arrive at least 30 minutes prior to your departure time at Island Adventure Whale Watching, located at 115 East Railroad Avenue, Port Angeles, WA 98362. Check in at the *Whale Watching Loading Zone* at the top of the ramp. A crew member will then check you in and guide you to the boat at the dock. It is imperative that you be on time, as the boat will leave promptly at the scheduled departure time.

- Recommended parking can be found across the street at 150 East Front Street
- Arrive 30 minutes prior to departure
- No need for paperwork
- Bring layers, sunglasses and sunscreen
- Remember your credit or debit card
- *Be sure to bring your camera or binoculars*

☐ Feiro Marine Life Center

About a block east of the Black Ball Ferry Line Terminal is the small Feiro Marine Life Center. Here, visitors can peruse displays and talk with the staff to learn about the fish, mollusks, invertebrates and other marine life that inhabit the waters of the North

Olympic Peninsula, as well as reach into the many touch tanks for an up close experience. *If you're lucky and the timing is right*, they may even have a Giant Pacific Octopus as a resident!

Admission: $5.00 for Adults, $4.00 for Seniors, and $3.00 for youth ages 3 to 17.

> Feiro Marine Life Center
> 315 North Lincoln Street
> Port Angeles, WA 98362
> 360-417-6254

- Open:
    - Summer: Daily: 10:00 a.m. to 5:00 p.m.
    - Winter: Daily - 12:00 p.m. to 5:00 p.m.

☐ Museum at the Carnegie

Housed in a distinct historical building that is one of the oldest in Port Angeles, the Museum at the Carnegie tells of the history of the area through artifacts, displays, photos, and documents featured in seven permanent exhibits. Here, you'll learn about the Clallam tribe and their ancestral heritage, the first non-Native American settlers to the area, the formation of Olympic National Park, the different industries of the region, the maritime history of the area, and more.

There is no admission fee to the museum, but a small donation of $5 per person is suggested.

> Museum at the Carnegie
> 205 South Lincoln Street
> Port Angeles, WA 98362
> 360-452-6779

- Open:
  - Tuesday through Friday - 1:00 p.m. to 4:00 p.m.
  - Saturday - 12:00 p.m. to 2:00 p.m.
  - Closed Sunday and Monday

 ☐ **Port Angeles Underground Heritage Tour**

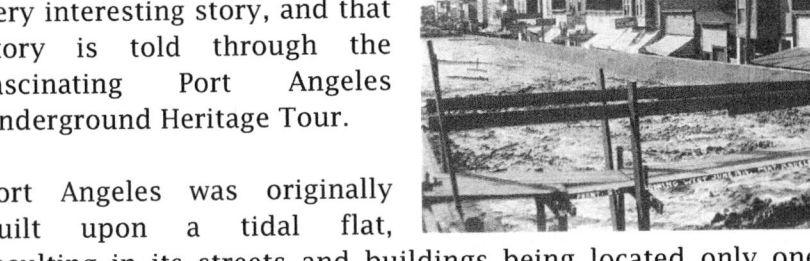

The history of Port Angeles' downtown area makes for a very interesting story, and that story is told through the fascinating Port Angeles Underground Heritage Tour.

Port Angeles was originally built upon a tidal flat, resulting in its streets and buildings being located only one foot or so above sea level. Unfortunately, this meant that every time a significantly high tide came in, the streets and buildings of Port Angeles would flood. Beginning in January of 1914, the city fathers decided to raise the streets, *but not the buildings*, anywhere from 6' to 15' in a complex engineering feat that involved building tall concrete walls alongside four downtown streets and then filling the streets with mud that was sluiced from the hillside above town up to the top of the concrete walls. Once completed, the buildings on each side of the raised streets, which were now 6' to 15' *below* street level, were raised one at a time upon massive cedar post foundations, thus creating an extensive underground network of buried storefronts, sidewalks, and darkened passageways below.

Take the guided 2 hour Port Angeles Underground Heritage Tour to learn the captivating story about how the streets were raised, and then drop below and tour the historical world beneath the streets of Port Angeles.

All tours meet at and depart from behind the Port Angeles Information Center located at 121 East Railroad Avenue in downtown Port Angeles. Look for the signs behind the Information Center that lead you through the double doors on the lower level of Smuggler's Landing and you'll see the meeting area immediately to your right. Reservations are not required, but are appreciated. Note that there are several flights of stairs on this tour.

Schedule:

Tours occur Monday through Saturday at 2:00 p.m., year-round. Group tours may also be arranged for anytime by calling 360-808-2544.

Rates:

Adult: $15.00
Distinguished Adult (60+): $12.00
Student (13+): $12.00
Child (6-12): $8.00
Children under 6 are free.

Port Angeles Underground Heritage Tour
Port Angeles, WA 98362
360-808-2544

www.Discover-Washington.com

☐ Family Shoe Store - Oldest Building in Downtown Port Angeles

Built in 1890, the Family Shoe Store at 130 W Front Street (Look for the big red goose painted on the side of the building) is the oldest surviving structure in downtown Port Angeles. Today, it is home to a shoe store, but at one time its second floor was a hotel and brothel hosting sailors who called on Port Angeles from around the world. Visitors on the Port Angeles Underground Heritage Tour may visit the upstairs, which has a collection of rooms that have been furnished with vintage furniture to give a representation of how the "hotel" appeared in its heyday. Note that these rooms are not open to the public and may be viewed only as part of the tour.

Family Shoe Store
130 W Front Street
Port Angeles, WA 98362
360-452-3741

☐ Dungeness Crab & Seafood Festival

Every October, Port Angeles celebrates the culinary delight that is the Dungeness Crab in the fun, festive, and *delicious* 3-day Dungeness Crab & Seafood Festival.

Located on the Port Angeles waterfront, the festival features over a dozen local restaurants offering an abundance of fresh crab, seafood, beer, and wine. Choose a full crab, half crab, crab cakes, crab rolls, crab cocktails...if it's made with Dungeness Crab, you'll find it at the festival. You'll also find delicious shrimp, clams, mussels and a bounty of other fresh seafood, all prepared in a variety of tasty dishes.

When you've finished your meal(s), take a stroll to enjoy cooking demonstrations, the Grab-A-Crab Derby, crab races, local vendors and artisans, live music, and much more!

You'll find the festival with its many large tents on the waterfront at Port Angeles, at the foot of Lincoln Street and Railroad Avenue. The festival occurs rain or shine every early to mid-October, and the admission is free.

Getting Low On Gas?

If you're planning on venturing west from Port Angeles to some of the more remote locations on the peninsula, you may find it convenient to fill your tank in Port Angeles where there are many gas stations to choose from. While gas is available sporadically further out west, you won't have as many choices as you do here.

www.Discover-Washington.com

Notes

www.Discover-Washington.com

Olympic Mountains – Olympic National Park

LAKE CRESCENT, SOL DUC & OLYMPIC NATIONAL PARK

Lake Crescent Area

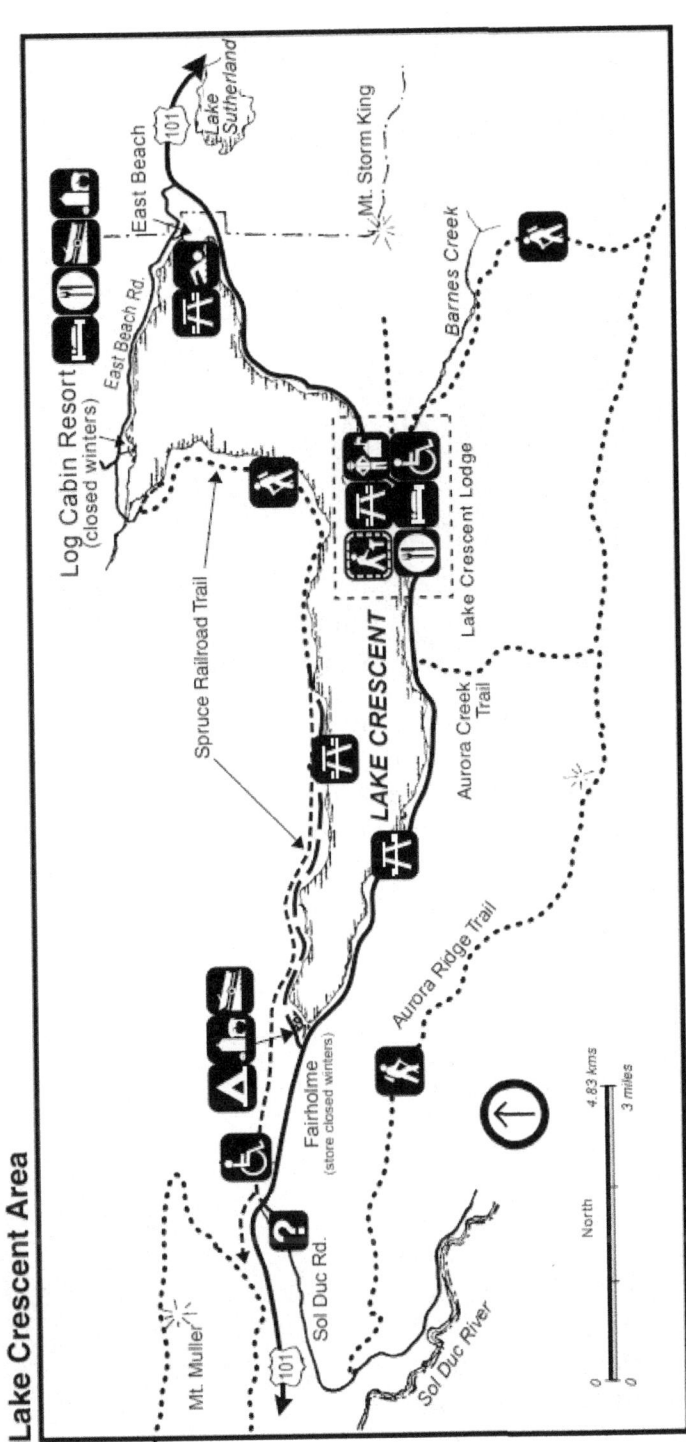

Lake Crescent

Resting at the base of the majestic Olympic Mountains, scenic Lake Crescent welcomes its visitors with an abundance of activities. Explore its shores while looking for colorful birdlife, hike through its mossy old growth forests of towering fir and cedar trees to a delightful waterfall, rent a small rowboat or canoe to cast a fly for a trout in its clear waters, or simply find a place to sit, relax, and enjoy the lake's captivating scenery and many moods.

☐ Storm King Ranger Station

A little ways east of Lake Crescent Lodge is an interesting cabin at the edge of a small meadow on the shore of the lake. This is the historic 1905 Storm King Ranger Station. More a museum than a ranger station, the cabin has no official public purpose and

is open only intermittently during the summer months, and closed during the rest of the year.

To reach the cabin, follow the exit road from Lake Crescent Lodge south and then east to the 4-way stop. Continue straight to the obvious parking area and find the Storm King Ranger Station in the meadow nearby.

 ☐ **Marymere Falls**

This popular hike takes visitors through a pleasant old-growth forest of towering cedar and fir trees, as well as some impressive big leaf maples, before arriving at beautiful Marymere Falls. Surrounded by lush greenery, it drops 90' from a notch in the rock above before splashing into a log-strewn pool below.

The gravel and dirt trail is a little over 1.5 miles in length round-trip and it takes between 30 to 45 minutes to reach the falls. You'll cross two bridges before ascending a set of four switchbacks with steps up to the base of the falls. As an option, you can also take a steep loop trail up to the mid-section of the falls.

From Lake Crescent Lodge, follow the exit road south and then east to the 4-way stop. Continue straight to the obvious parking area and find the Storm King Ranger Station in the nearby meadow. The trailhead for Marymere Falls is located in front of the ranger station. Note that no pets are allowed on the trail.

www.Discover-Washington.com

☐ Moments in Time Trail & Barnes Point

This family friendly 0.6 mile self-guided interpretive trail meanders through an old growth forest lush with moss and ferns as it explains the historical, geological, and ecological importance of the Lake Crescent area.

There are several entry and exit points along the trail as it makes its way by Lake Crescent's shore. Look for a trailhead at the Storm King Ranger Station, as well as Lake Crescent Lodge.

 ## ☐ Spruce Railroad Trail

During World War I, Sitka spruce wood was in demand for building aircraft. Lightweight, yet very strong and easy to work with, it is the standard by which all other woods are measured when it comes to building aircraft, and the Olympic Peninsula was rich with Sitka spruce stands that grew well in the wet climate near the Pacific Ocean. In 1918, work began on the Spruce Railroad line, which would allow for the quick and efficient removal of harvested Sitka spruce trees. Passing along the northern shore of Lake Crescent, the line was to continue to Port Angeles, where the trees would be shipped out to help the war effort. Though the war ended before the line was finished, it was eventually completed and used to move trees cut for commercial purposes until it was abandoned in 1951.

Today, that former railway is undergoing an impressive multi-year improvement project to create a year-round multi-use trail shared by hikers, cyclists, equestrians, and those in wheelchairs, all as part of the larger plan to create the

Olympic Discovery Trail, a 130 mile route stretching across the northern Olympic Peninsula from Port Townsend to La Push.

Take the time while exploring Lake Crescent to hike the first mile of the level Spruce Railroad Trail from the East Beach trailhead out to Devil's Punchbowl. Here, a long footbridge spans a small cove along the north shore of Lake Crescent, which is a very popular swimming and diving hole in the summer due to its depth of over 100'. Along the way, you'll enjoy views of the lake, as well as its crystal clear waters. Note that the Spruce Railroad Trail is one of the few trails of its kind in any National Park that allows dogs and bikes.

Directions: From Lake Crescent Lodge, return east on Hwy 101 to East Beach Road at the east end of the lake. Turn left at the large sign that reads *Olympic National Park - East Beach - Log Cabin Resort* and follow this narrow road for 3.2 miles to where you'll see a sign for the Spruce Railroad Trail. Turn left here and proceed another mile to the trailhead.

 ☐ **Lake Crescent Boat Tours**

Set out on a unique adventure to learn about Lake Crescent and the amazing natural, cultural and geological history of the area aboard the new Lake Crescent Scenic Boat Tour. Depart from the boat dock in front of the lodge and spend 1.5 hours on the water as you make your way around the entire lake. Tours depart three to five times a day on Thursdays through Sundays during the summer months. Visit the front desk of the Lake Crescent Lodge to make your reservation and to inquire about suggested weather-dependent attire for your tour.

- Adults: $27.00
- Children under 16: $13.00
- Children under 30 lbs.: Free

Hurricane Ridge at Olympic National Park

High Ridge Trail - Hurricane Ridge

Leave sea level and set out to explore Hurricane Ridge at nearly 5,500' high, where you'll take in sweeping views of the Olympic Mountains, capped by snowy Mt. Olympus at 7,980'.

Stop in at the Hurricane Ridge Visitor Center, stroll through a high alpine meadow, hear the shrill call of a marmot, and hike a trail or two to a nearby summit.

Directions: From South Race Street in Port Angeles, follow Hurricane Ridge Road south for 17 miles as it climbs to the Hurricane Ridge Visitor Center. Note that a National Park Pass is required to enter the park, and you may purchase one of these at the small entrance kiosk located approximately 5.5 miles up the road. *This permit is valid for seven consecutive days, so be sure to keep your receipt, as it may be used elsewhere while visiting Olympic National Park.*

Note that Hurricane Ridge Road is open daily throughout the summer months, but is open only Friday though Sunday, as well as holiday Mondays, during the winter months, weather and road conditions permitting. All vehicles climbing Hurricane Ridge Road to the Visitor Center during the winter months must carry tire chains. To get an update on the status of Hurricane Ridge Road, as well as the current hours of the Visitor Center, call 360-565-3131.

☐ Hurricane Ridge Visitor Center

Drive up Hurricane Ridge Road directly to the Hurricane Ridge Visitor Center, where you'll find interesting exhibits about the natural and cultural history  of the Olympic Mountains and the Olympic Peninsula. Grab a bite to eat in the snack bar and then sit a while on the large stone patio outside to enjoy the commanding view of the Olympic Mountains in the distance.

Hurricane Ridge Visitor Center
3002 Mt. Angeles Road
Port Angeles, WA 98362
360-565-3131

- Open: Daily during the summer months – 8:30 a.m. to 5:00 p.m. Hours vary during the winter months. To get an update on the current hours of the Visitor Center, call 360-565-3131. Note that a web cam for checking the conditions at Hurricane Ridge is available online.

www.Discover-Washington.com

☐ Take a Hike on Hurricane Ridge

Choose from three different trails departing from the Hurricane Ridge Visitor Center, each offering captivating views and a high alpine experience.

Big Meadow Trail

A short paved 0.25 mile trail near the parking area takes you through open alpine meadows.

Cirque Rim Trail

This paved 0.75 mile trail winds its way along a ridge north of the parking area and offers views of Port Angeles, the Strait of Juan de Fuca, and even Canada in the far distance.

High Ridge Trail

This steep trail quickly ascends from the east end of the parking area to take you to Sunrise Point, along a high ridge, and through alpine meadows. From your lofty traverse, you'll spot the Strait of Juan de Fuca, Canada, the Cascade Mountains, the Olympic Mountains, and more as you make your way along this high trail dotted with open meadows, alpine firs, marmots, chipmunks, and deer.

Note that pets and bikes are not allowed on these trails.

www.Discover-Washington.com

Sol Duc River Area

Located in a lush green forest at the west end of Lake Crescent, the Sol Duc River Area offers visitors a refreshing soak in a large pool fed by hot springs, as well as one of the more dramatic waterfalls in all of Olympic National Park.

☐ Sol Duc Hot Springs Resort & Pool

Located near the end of Hot Springs Road, the Sol Duc Hot Springs Resort offers guests the opportunity to soak away the stress of the day in their large pools fed by hot mineral springs. Afterwards, enjoy a massage, have a meal, and consider returning to stay in one of the resort's many cabins.

☐ Sol Duc Falls

Perhaps the most impressive waterfall within Olympic National Park, especially during the spring months when the Sol Duc River swells with snowmelt, the four fingers of Sol Duc Falls roar as they fall 48 feet into a narrow rocky chasm below, thundering as mist swirls high into the air.

From the trailhead at the end of Sol Duc Road, follow the wide well-maintained gravel trail through an old-growth forest for 0.8 mile to a bridge spanning Sol Duc River and nearby viewing platforms for the falls.

Notes

www.Discover-Washington.com

Elwha River, Joyce, Clallam Bay & Sekiu

Elwha River Area

The Elwha River area marks the beginning of the more remote section of the northern Olympic Peninsula. Here, the Strait of Juan de Fuca Scenic Byway leads you westward on a sinuous course as it tracks closer to the strait, tempting you with countless opportunities to pull over and enjoy the beauty...*and there's no reason why you shouldn't!*

Note: You can find gas in Joyce, Clallam Bay, and Sappho, at the junction of Hwy 101 and Hwy 113.

☐ Madison Creek Falls – Elwha River

Not far off of Hwy 101 is the small yet beautiful Madison Creek Falls. Tucked into a lush green alcove, it falls and cascades down a mossy rock face for 50 feet before flowing as a small stream through the forest to the Elwha River. The year-round path to the falls is paved, level, and requires only a few minutes to traverse. You will find restrooms here.

To reach the falls, turn south from Hwy 101 onto Olympic Hot Springs Road immediately east of the Elwha River, 11.5 miles east of Lake Crescent. Follow the road along the Elwha River until you see the parking area for the falls on your left.

www.Discover-Washington.com

☐ Elwha River Observation Area

In 1992, Congress passed the Elwha River Ecosystem and Fisheries Restoration Act, which authorized the removal of two large dams on the Elwha River. Two decades later, on September 17, 2011, the largest dam removal project ever to occur in the United States began with the removal of Elwha Dam, followed with the removal of the Glines Canyon Dam upriver in 2014.

Visit the site of the Elwha Dam removal and marvel at the fact that it simply appears to be a free-flowing river through a rocky canyon...which was exactly the goal of the dam removal.

The Elwha River Observation Area consists of two components;

1) The Elwha River Restoration Interpretive Center, which is an open structure that tells the story of the construction of the two dams and their ultimate removal, as well as the positive ecological effects of returning the Elwha River to its free-flowing state.

2) The former dam site itself.

Directions: From Hwy 101, turn north onto Hwy 112, the Strait of Juan de Fuca Scenic Byway, and in 0.7 mile turn south onto Lower Dam Road. Look for the sign for the Interpretive Center structure, which is on your right, tucked into the trees just beyond a bend in the short road.

To reach the former dam site, park in the *Elwha Dam Viewpoint* parking area opposite of where you turned onto the road for the Interpretive Center structure and park in the parking area immediately on your right, prior to entering the Elwha Dam RV Park. You may take a small trail located on the left side of the parking area or opt to hike down Lower Dam Road, which begins to the right of the parking area. The small trail will take you to a wooded observation area, which doesn't offer much in the way of a view, but you can take a short trail from there to Lower Dam Road, which continues downhill for approximately ¼ mile to the former dam site.

Elwha River Restoration Interpretive Center
61 Lower Dam Road
Port Angles, WA 98363

☐ Elwha Beach

Elwha Beach is known as one of the Olympic Peninsula's best kept secrets, and it keeps this secret right up until you reach the beach itself.

With the removal of the Elwha Dam, all of the sediment behind the dam washed down

to the mouth of the Elwha River and in turn created a long sandy beach, which is somewhat of a rarity on the north shore of the Olympic Peninsula. Park your car in the small parking area, stroll out the gravel pathway for about 1/8th of a mile, and then discover all that this beach has to offer. Walk its shoreline as you gaze out over the waters of the Strait of Juan

de Fuca, keep an eye out for whales, sea lions, and other sea life, watch the bald eagles that soar overhead, start a clam shell collection, or find a seat on one of the many large logs that are scattered along the shoreline and watch the surfers catch a wave. (During the spring and fall months) This is a great spot to sit for a while and enjoy the Olympic Peninsula's ocean environment.

Directions: From the Elwha River Observation Area, drive directly across Hwy 112 to Power Plant Road and follow this to Laird Road. Turn left / north here and follow this as it curves to the east. In ½ mile after the curve turn left / north onto Lower Elwha Road and follow this for 2.6 miles as it winds its way toward the strait and the parking area for Elwha Beach.

☐ Elwha River Bridge

As you make your way back to Hwy 112, you'll pass over the Elwha River Bridge, an impressive engineering feat you'll want to stop and appreciate. Park off the pavement at the west end of the bridge and walk down the obvious path to the bridge's lower deck. Part of the Olympic Discovery Trail, the suspended lower deck connects the trail over the Elwha River below, allowing cyclists and pedestrians to safely cross the river while cars and trucks pass overhead.

Directions: From Elwha Beach, return on Lower Elwha Road to W Edgewood Drive. Turn right / west here and follow this as it curves south and becomes Laird Road. (This is the way you came.) In a short distance, turn right / west onto Elwha River Road and follow this to the bridge. After you visit the bridge, simply continue west on Elwha River Road and you can reconnect with Hwy 112.

www.Discover-Washington.com

☐ Kayaking Freshwater Bay

From high alpine mountaineering in the rugged Olympic Mountains to SCUBA diving in the deep Salish Sea, the Olympic Peninsula offers a wealth of outdoor activities and adventures.

Set out on an exciting sea kayaking tour with Adventures Through Kayaking to explore Freshwater Bay and the surrounding shoreline, 11 miles west of Port Angeles. Launching out from shore with your experienced guide, you'll find yourself now a part of the ocean environment as you quietly paddle along the shore of the Strait of Juan de Fuca while scanning the cliffsides, sea stacks, sea caves and open waters for marine life, including otters, seals, sea lions, jellyfish, and an abundance of birds. And because you're along the whale trail, you may even spot the spout of a gray whale or a pod of orcas!

Beginners are more than welcome to enjoy this tour, as it is suitable for most people. Note that you will want to have a good deal of endurance in case you encounter a headwind while returning to the launch point, which can sometimes occur, though your guide will take this into consideration.

Available: April through September – Tours go out at **9:00 a.m.** and **1:30 p.m.**

Plan for the entire excursion to take 4 hours, with 2.5 hours spent on the water. The check-in location for your kayak tour is at Adventures Through Kayaking, located at 2358 West, Hwy 101, which is east of Hwy 101's junction with Hwy 112.

Adventures Through Kayaking
2358 West, US-101
Port Angeles, WA 98363
360-417-3015
www.atkayaking.com

☐ Joyce Museum & General Store

The rich history of the Joyce, Lake Crescent, and Twin Rivers area is preserved for visitors to discover and enjoy at the fascinating Joyce Museum. Housed in a sturdy 1914 train depot built of logs, the museum showcases carefully curated artifacts depicting life on the northern Olympic Peninsula at the turn of the prior century. Photos, books, household items, tools from the construction of the Elwha Dam, even a well-preserved 1890 Studebaker runabout horse carriage all await inspection by a modern day traveler.

You'll find the Joyce Museum next door to the Joyce General Store, a friendly market and Post Office offering an abundant selection of snacks, drinks, and other items for your trip, as well as gas and restrooms.

Joyce Museum & General Store
50883 Highway 112
Port Angeles, WA 98363
360-928-3568

- Open:
    - Summer: Thursday through Monday – 10:00 a.m. to 4:00 p.m.
    - Winter: Friday through Sunday – 10:00 a.m. to 4:00 p.m.

☐ Pillar Point Recreation Area

As you drive west on the Strait of Juan de Fuca Scenic Byway, you begin catching glimpses of the water between the trees. Like Freshwater Bay, Pillar Point is a perfect spot at which to stop and watch for whales, spot a variety of shore birds, and gaze out over the wide expanse of the Strait of Juan de Fuca at the passing freighters in the distance. Enjoy the beautiful scenery from the comfort of your car or find a log to sit upon along the rocky shoreline.

You'll find the Pillar Point Recreation area a little over 21 miles west of Joyce and just before reaching the small town of Pysht. Look for Pillar Point Road on the north side of Hwy 101 and travel this a short distance to Pillar Point.

☐ Roosevelt Elk Herds

A little more than 5 miles west of Pysht, Hwy 112 connects with Hwy 113. If you turn north here and *continue on Hwy 112*, the Strait of Juan de Fuca Scenic Byway for 3.9 miles, you'll see a field on your right, and if you're lucky you'll spot a large herd of 40 or more elk grazing here. Note that if you don't see the elk here, you may spot them in other fields along Hwy 112.

www.Discover-Washington.com

☐ Clallam Bay Visitors Center

Stop in at the Clallam Bay Visitor Center to learn all about the Clallam Bay and Sekiu areas, the nearby tide pools at Slip Point, and Clallam Bay State Park next door.

Clallam Bay Visitors Center
16753 Hwy 112
Clallam Bay, WA 98326
360-963-2339

- Open: Daily - April through October – 10:00 a.m. to 3:00 p.m., Hours can vary during the winter months.

☐ Clallam Bay State Park

When visiting Clallam Bay, take a moment to explore Clallam Bay State Park. Walk the short paved path from the parking area over the footbridge to the beach and be sure to bring your binoculars, as the park is one of the prime viewing spots along the Great Washington State Birding Trail.

www.Discover-Washington.com

☐ Tide Pools at Slip Point on Clallam Bay

Just east of Clallam Bay State Park are the tide pools of Slip Point, the easternmost point of the bay. Here, you'll find an abundance of mussels, sea urchins, small crabs, giant acorn barnacles, sea otters, eagles and more. It's also fun to look through the flotsam and jetsam lining the shore as you walk to and from the point. In case you're wondering, those concrete piers you see here used to support a wooden catwalk that led to the Slip Point Lighthouse.

Directions: Park at Clallam Bay State Park and take the trail leading west from the parking area across the small bridge and out to the shoreline. From here, walk east along the pebbly beach to Slip Point.

Note that you MUST be mindful of the tide. Visit Slip Point *only when the tide is out and still retreating*. Note, as well, that the large rocks closer to shore can be surprisingly slippery.

Slip Point Lighthouse photo © Kraig Anderson - LighthouseFriends.com

www.Discover-Washington.com

☐ Shipwreck Point

Located less than a mile west of Chito Beach Resort (7639 Highway 112) is the Shipwreck Point Natural Resources Conservation Area, a 472-acre forest fronted by a 3 mile stretch of beach. Part of the "Whale Trail", this portion of the Strait of Juan de Fuca is a great place to watch for passing gray whales, humpbacks, and orcas. In addition, keen observers may spot harbor seals and sea otters swimming among the kelp beds off shore.

You'll find a small roadside pullout with an interpretive sign for Shipwreck Point 1.2 miles west of Chito Beach Resort on the Strait of Juan de Fuca Scenic Byway.

www.Discover-Washington.com

NOTES

www.Discover-Washington.com

Cape Flattery Lighthouse

Neah Bay, Cape Flattery & Shi Shi Beach

Neah Bay

The busy fishing village of Neah Bay is home to the fascinating Makah Cultural & Research Center Museum and next door to scenic Cape Flattery, the northwestern most point of land on the Olympic Peninsula, as well as the contiguous United States.

Important:

Note that in order to park at, visit or access public recreation sites within the Makah Reservation, such as Cape Flattery, Shi Shi Beach, Hobuck Beach, and others, all visitors must purchase and display within their vehicle a Makah Tribe Recreational Use Permit. These annual permits may be purchased for $10 at a number of locations in Neah Bay and elsewhere, including Washburn's General Store, Makah Mini Mart, Makah Marina, Hobuck Beach Resort and the Makah Cultural & Research Center Museum. You'll find the Makah Museum to be a convenient location at which to purchase a permit.

☐ Makah Cultural & Research Center Museum

Over 500 years ago, a massive landslide buried six longhouses of a Makah village, encasing thousands of wood-based artifacts in a protective shroud of mud, thus preserving the items. In 1969, a storm caused a bank at the village to slump, and in doing so exposed many of these perfectly preserved artifacts. In time, over 55,000 pieces were discovered at the site, and today the Makah Museum tells the story behind these pieces through an intriguing display of exhibits containing weavings, baskets, canoes, carvings, tools, attire, photographs, a longhouse, and more, all providing a rare glimpse into the life of the Makah tribe in this area over 500 years ago.

Admission:

- Adult: $6.00
- Student & Senior Citizen: $5.00
- Makah: Free

Makah Museum
1880 Bayview Ave.
Neah Bay, WA 98357
360-645-2711

- Open: Daily – 10:00 a.m. to 5:00 p.m.

www.Discover-Washington.com

Cape Flattery

If the weather is good and the sun is out, then the hike to Cape Flattery is an impressive and memorable highlight of your trip to the northern Olympic Peninsula!

Located on the Makah Indian Reservation, the 0.7 mile Cape Flattery Trail leads travelers along a well-maintained path winding through the forest to Cape Flattery, the northwestern most point of land in the contiguous 48 states. Here, multiple viewing platforms offer commanding views out over the Strait of Juan de Fuca, as well as the rocky caverns and bays below. Take the time to visit them all, but finish at the large observation deck at the end of the trail, overlooking the cape, the Strait of Juan de Fuca, Tatoosh Island, and the 1857 Cape Flattery Lighthouse. If the weather is nice, plan to spend some time here enjoying the view and looking for eagles, sea lions, sea otters, orcas, and even gray whales, which have been known to scavenge in the deep coves immediately below you. Oh, and don't forget your binoculars.

Drive Hwy 112 west through Neah Bay and follow the signs to Cape Flattery via the Cape Flattery Scenic Byway, which is reached in approximately 8 miles from town. Park at the trailhead and take the obvious trail that leads into a particularly interesting forest of contorted cedar trees. If ever there was a "haunted forest", this would be it. Continue hiking across multiple raised cedar planked boardwalks for approximately 15 minutes until you reach the first of the overlooks.

We recommend that you wear shoes on this hike, as there are a lot of roots in the second half of the trail, and it can be somewhat muddy after a recent rain. In addition, be sure to display your Makah Tribe Recreational Use Permit within your vehicle. (Page 133)

☐ Hobuck Beach

A large sandy beach offers visitors an opportunity to swim, surf, camp, or just go for a long walk near the waves while watching a beautiful sunset signal the end of another adventurous day.

Directions: Drive Hwy 112 west through Neah Bay and follow the Cape Flattery Scenic Byway signs toward Cape Flattery. At approximately 2.5 miles from Neah Bay, turn left onto Hobuck Road and follow this across the Wa'atch River to the Makah Passage road. Turn right here and find Hobuck Beach in approximately 1/2 mile.

Shi Shi Beach

  Picturesque Shi Shi Beach is extremely popular with beach campers and backpackers alike who traverse the 2 mile Shi Shi Beach Trail to stay overnight on the coast or continue south to the Point of Arches, which many consider to be one of the most beautiful beaches on the entire Olympic Peninsula, with its mile-long collection of dramatic sea stacks standing in the surf just off shore.

The well-traveled Shi Shi Beach Trail meanders its way through a shady coastal forest for its first mile, crossing cedar plank boardwalks and bridges before traversing an old overgrown road for the second mile. Note that this second half of the trail has many sections which are often quite wet and muddy. However, dry side trails up on the banks around these sections can usually be found, sometimes leading as far as 20' away from the "main" trail, so keep an eye out for them. Shortly after you begin to hear the surf through the trees, you'll come upon an "entrance" to Olympic National Park, (it's just a trail sign) where you'll then drop down a short but very steep section of trail to Shi Shi Beach below. Here, you'll find a long and scenic sandy beach littered with logs and driftwood  stretching for miles to the south. Find a place to sit and enjoy the view, explore some sea stacks and tide pools nearby, or choose to take off your shoes and hike south for a little over 2 miles to the Point of Arches.

- Distance to Shi Shi Beach: 2 Miles (4 Miles roundtrip)
- Distance to Point of Arches: 4 Miles (8 Miles roundtrip)
- Plan on hiking 1 hour each way at a moderate pace for the 2 mile hike
- Plan on 3 hours total, if you spend 1 hour on the beach
- Be sure to bring water, sunglasses and sunscreen
- A Makah Tribe Recreation Use Permit is required to park at the Shi Shi Beach trailhead – See page 133

Directions: Drive Hwy 112 west through Neah Bay and follow the Cape Flattery Scenic Byway signs toward Cape Flattery. Instead of continuing to Cape Flattery, turn left onto Hobuck Road at approximately 2.5 miles from Neah Bay and follow the signs to the Shi Shi Beach Trailhead at 4.3 miles.

www.Discover-Washington.com

NOTES

www.Discover-Washington.com

Lake Ozette, Rialto Beach, Forks, & The Hoh Rainforest

Lake Ozette Area

Like Shi Shi Beach, Lake Ozette and the ocean beaches nearby are very popular with car campers, beach campers and backpackers. Choose from 15 year-round campsites at Lake Ozette or hike one of two trails out to the coast to stay the night...or two or three. Ambitious hikers can combine the two 3 mile trails and a 3 mile section of the coast to make a loop that is a little over 9 miles in length.

Directions: Turn south onto Hoko-Ozette Road/Ozette Lake Road 16 miles *east* of Neah Bay and follow the signs to the Ozette Ranger Station, where you'll find the single trailhead for two popular hikes near the large interpretive "kiosk" behind the ranger station. Take this trail through the forest for a short distance to where it splits in two for the Sand Point and Cape Alava trails.

Sand Point Trail – Hike 3 miles on raised cedar plank boardwalks through a lowland coastal forest of deciduous and fir trees, as well as dense undergrowth to Sand Point, which is south of Cap Alava.

Cape Alava Trail – This 3.1 mile hike takes you through dense undergrowth of salal, licorice ferns, skunk cabbage and other lowland plants that thrive in this damp coastal environment, all crowding the raised cedar plank boardwalks that lead to beautiful Cape Alava.

www.Discover-Washington.com

Rialto Beach

Journey out to La Push to find Rialto Beach, a beautiful stretch of coast lined with large driftwood logs and more skipping stones than you've ever seen in your life!

Directions: Turn off of Hwy 101 onto Hwy 110 and follow this west toward La Push. Turn right onto Mora Road at the 3 Rivers Resort, where you can find gas, and follow this directly to Rialto Beach.

Forks, WA

☐ John's Beachcombing Museum

You know how fun it is to find something interesting that has floated up on shore? Well imagine finding thousands of interesting things! For over 40 years, John Anderson has been collecting "treasures from around the world" that have washed up on shore, and he presents them all in John's Beachcombing Museum. Stop in to see countless different items, including glass and plastic fishing floats, light bulbs of all shapes and sizes, signs, hardhats, toothbrushes, notes in glass bottles, parts from old sailing vessels, and even a large iron chain from the 1500s.

John's Beachcombing Museum
143 Andersonville Ave.
Forks, WA 98331
360-640-0320

(Look for the large sign for the museum on your right *north of town* as you drive south into Forks on Hwy 101.)

- Open: Daily – Summer months - 10:00 a.m. to 5:00 p.m.

☐ Forever Twilight in Forks Collection

While the Twilight movie series wasn't filmed in Forks, the novels by Stephenie Meyer were based here, and this means Forks is celebrated as the center of the Twilight universe. Stop at the Forever Twilight in Forks Collection to talk all about Bella, Edward, and Jacob, as well as to see an impressive display of movie props and costumes, Twilight Saga novels from around the world and other interesting memorabilia.

Admission is free, but donations are gladly accepted.

Forever Twilight in Forks Collection
Rainforest Arts Center Alcove
11 N. Forks Avenue
Forks, WA 98331
360-374-2531

- Open: 12:00 p.m. to 4:00 p.m. – Thursday through Sunday

www.Discover-Washington.com

☐ Tillicum Park

Visit Tillicum Park just off Hwy 101 in Forks, WA to see the impressive Rayonier #10, an over 100 year-old Shay locomotive used for logging on the Olympic Peninsula.

☐ Forks Timber Museum

Timber has played a very important role in shaping the cultural and economic history of the Forks area, as well as the Olympic Peninsula. Stop at the Forks Timber Museum on the south end of town, sign their guest book, and then step inside to learn all about the history of timber logging in the area through a wealth of impressive exhibits, displays, photos, tools, artifacts and more. Oh, and be sure to visit the Visitor Center located right next door before you leave to learn all about the attractions in Forks and the surrounding area.

Forks Timber Museum
1421 S. Forks Ave.
Forks, WA 98331
360-374-9663

- Open: Monday through Saturday - 10:00 a.m. to 5:00 p.m., Sundays - 11:00 a.m. to 4:00 p.m.

www.Discover-Washington.com

Hoh Rainforest

☐ Hoh Rainforest & Trails

Receiving an impressive 12 to 14 *feet* of rainfall every year, the Hoh Rainforest lives up to its name with lush, green moss seemingly covering nearly every inch of the towering big leaf maples, western red cedars, and massive ancient Sitka spruce trees that grow here. Everywhere you look the branches and trunks from the forest floor to the upper canopy are draped in moss hanging in thick mats that look both beautiful and otherworldly.

To experience the Hoh Rainforest, we recommend two trails that leave from the Visitor Center:

Hoh River Trail – This is a 17.3 mile trail, but you'll want to hike only a short distance of it. While the forest is lush and green throughout the hike, at approximately the 0.5 mile mark the moss becomes especially thick, covering the big leaf maples in an abundance of moss mats.

Hall of Mosses – This 0.8 mile loop trail crosses a small surprisingly clear stream before ascending a steep 100' rise up to a level plateau. From here, it meanders through the trees as interpretive signs along the way explain the ecosystem of this temperate old-growth rain forest.

The Quietest Place in the United States

Take the time to hike 3.2 miles up the Hoh River Trail and you'll spot on your left an oddly shaped Sitka spruce tree that you could walk through on a small path. Follow this pathway north for approximately 200 yards and you'll find yourself standing in what is actually known as the quietest place in the United States. In 1984, Gordon Hempton of Port Angeles began a quest to discover the one location that exists anywhere undisturbed by any sounds created by man, be it road noise, habitation, construction, or even aircraft overhead. His research determined that the quietest place in the United States actually exists relatively close to his home, in the Hoh Rainforest of Olympic National Park. Listen carefully, and while you may hear the wind rushing through the trees or perhaps the call of a Steller's Jay, you won't hear any sounds in this unique location created by human activity.

Directions to the Hoh Rainforest in Olympic National Park: Travel south on Hwy 101 for 13 miles south of Forks and turn left / east onto Upper Hoh Road. Follow this for 18 miles directly to the Hoh Rain Forest Visitor Center.

www.Discover-Washington.com

Northwest Olympic Peninsula Restaurants

As you make your way west beyond Port Angeles, dining options become fewer. In addition, many restaurants are not open every day, and their closing hours can be a bit fluid and dependent upon how busy they are. Expect reduced hours during the winter months.

Below is a list of *some* of the restaurants in the more remote northwest section of the northern Olympic Peninsula.

By the Bay Café (Photo)
343 Front Street
Sekiu, WA 98381
360-963-2998

Open: Wednesday through Saturday – 7:00 a.m. to 9:00 p.m., Sunday – 7:00 a.m. to 8:00 p.m.

Breakwater Restaurant
15582 Hwy 112
Clallam Bay, WA 98326
360-963-2428

Open: Monday, Wednesday and Thursday – 8:00 a.m. to 9:00 p.m., Friday and Saturday – 8:00 a.m. to 10:00 p.m., and Tuesday – 11:00 a.m. to 9:00 p.m.

Pat's Place
931 Bayview Avenue
Neah Bay, WA 98357

Open: Tuesday through Saturday – 11:00 a.m. to 6:00 p.m. or 7:00 p.m., depending upon how busy they are.

Linda's Woodfired Kitchen
1110 Bay View Ave.
Neah Bay, WA 98357
360-640-2192

Open: Hours vary, but are generally Tuesday thru Sunday – 6:30 a.m. to 10:00 a.m. and 2:00 p.m. to 8:00 p.m.

Hungry Bear Café
205912 US-101
Beaver, WA 98305
(2 Miles east of Sappho)
360-327-3225

Open: Daily – 9:00 a.m. to 7:00 p.m. or 8:00 p.m., depending upon how busy they are.

(Yep, that's our car parked in front!)

www.Discover-Washington.com

Historic Hotels on the Northern Olympic Peninsula

The northern Olympic Peninsula is rich in cultural and maritime history, and what better way to immerse yourself in the essence of that history than staying in a unique historic hotel or B&B when making an overnight trip to the peninsula? With that in mind, here are 16 of our favorites...

Port Townsend

The Palace Hotel

Built of brick in 1889, the charming Palace Hotel in Port Townsend greets guests with a warm welcome after a day of travel. Step into the lobby and you begin to sense the colorful history of the building, all captured with nice Victorian era touches and refined details. Helpful staff will check you in before you make your way upstairs to your well-appointed period-specific rooms.

Since the hotel is located on Water Street, you're within walking distance for many attractions, including restaurants, coffee shops, tea houses, a theatre, museums, art galleries, boutiques, waterfront views and more.

The Palace Hotel
1004 Water Street
Port Townsend, WA 98368
360-385-0773

The Bishop Victorian Hotel

With its historical presence and Victorian charm, the 1890 Bishop Victorian Hotel stands alone on Washington Street, within easy walking distance to both downtown and uptown Port Townsend destinations.

You'll enjoy its quaint period-specific rooms, family friendly atmosphere, morning breakfast basket, and award-winning garden, perfect for a bit of relaxation after a day of exploring.

Bishop Victorian Hotel
714 Washington Street
Port Townsend, WA 98368
833-254-2469

The Waterstreet Hotel

Located in a large brick building downtown, The Waterstreet Hotel provides guests with a true sense of Port Townsend history. Here, instead of feeling overly "refurbished", the clean well-tended rooms feel more like one day has passed to the next since the hotel was first opened in 1889. If they're available, we recommend one of the rooms on the front corner of the hotel, overlooking Water Street.

The Waterstreet Hotel
635 Water Street
Port Townsend, WA 98368
360-385-5467

Manresa Castle Hotel

Located 5 minutes southwest of downtown Port Townsend, the large 1892 Manresa Castle Hotel affords a sense of elegance with its grand presence. Check in, ride the oldest operating elevator in Washington state up to your room and enjoy the views.

Manresa Castle Hotel
651 Cleveland Street
Port Townsend, WA 98368
360-385-5750

Old Consulate Inn

Voted Jefferson County's Best Bed & Breakfast, the beautiful 1889 Old Consulate Inn offers eight unique rooms with luxurious Victorian styling and views of Puget Sound, the Dimick Lighthouse home, and the Olympic Mountains.

Old Consulate Inn
313 Walker Street
Port Townsend, WA 98368
360-385-6753

www.Discover-Washington.com

FORT WORDEN

Alexander's Castle

Imagine staying overnight in your very own private castle!

Standing alone on the beautiful grounds of Fort Worden State Park is the oldest building at the fort, Alexander's Castle. Inside, the living room with a cozy gas fireplace, dining room, kitchen, 1.5 baths, and single master bedroom with a king bed upstairs capture the essence of 1883, yet with an overlay of modern luxury and amenities. Alexander's Castle offers a quiet stay, views of Puget Sound, and quick access to all of the hikes, views, museums and attractions found at Fort Worden. Note that the parking pass for Alexander's Castle, which you receive when you check in, also serves as your Discover Pass while in the State Park.

Alexander's Castle
262 Alexanders Loop
Port Townsend, WA 98368
360-344-4400

- Check in is at 4:00 p.m. in the Commons Building

- Learn more at www.FortWorden.org/stay-here/

www.Discover-Washington.com

Bliss Vista

If the opportunity is available, we highly recommend, in addition to Alexander's Castle, the small cottage known as Bliss Vista. Perhaps the most private of accommodations at Fort Worden, Bliss Vista provides guests with beautiful views of Puget Sound, Whidbey Island, the Point Wilson Lighthouse, Mt. Baker, passing ferries and more. Reservations may be made by calling 360-344-4434 or 360-344-4400.

Additional Lodging at Historic Fort Worden

In addition to Alexander's Castle and Bliss Vista, Fort Worden State Park offers 34 historical homes, cottages, apartment lofts, and the large Victorian homes of Officers Row for rent to the public, all in an open and beautiful "park like" setting. These accommodations can hold anywhere from 2 to 14 people, and reservations may be made by calling 360-344-4434 or visiting www.fortworden.org/stay-here/

www.Discover-Washington.com

Sequim & Port Angeles

George Washington Inn

History meets luxury at the stately George Washington Inn. Situated on a 10-acre estate of manicured grounds high on a bluff above the Strait of Juan de Fuca, the George Washington Inn welcomes visitors with views of the New Dungeness Lighthouse, Olympic National Park, and captivating romantic sunsets. Inside, guests are treated to luxury accommodations, spacious suites, private spa baths, and exceptional dining.

George Washington Inn
939 Finn Hall Road
Port Angeles, WA 98362
360-452-5207

Dungeness Barn House B&B

Gracious hosts Su and Clare welcome you to stay in the Dungeness Barn House B&B at Two Crows Farm, a beautifully restored historic barn on the edge of Dungeness Bay in Sequim. Four well-appointed rooms welcome guests with luxurious amenities that reflect your hosts' dedication to the guest experience and the attention to detail found throughout the property, from the well-manicured landscaping to the delicious breakfasts prepared with local farm fruits, vegetables, and herbs.

Dungeness Barn House B&B
42 Marine Drive
Sequim, WA 98382
360-582-1663

LAKE CRESCENT LODGE

Imagine a historic grand lodge over 100 years old tucked amongst towering old growth cedars and firs on the shores of a pristine mountain lake and you have Lake Crescent Lodge. Open since 1915, this classic lodge welcomes guests with a warm wood interior, Arts and Crafts style antique furniture, a large wood burning fireplace, and amazing views of Lake Crescent from a spacious enclosed porch, perfect for relaxing with a book or enjoying a slowly fading sunset after a day of exploration.

The lodge offers 38 rooms, as well as different options for cabins and cottages nearby, the most popular of which are the Roosevelt Fireplace Cabins,

which sit on the lake's shore. Note that the cabins may be reserved daily during the summer season and on weekends only, (Friday, Saturday and Sunday) January through April.

- Check-In: 4:00 p.m.
- Check-Out: 11:00 a.m.
- Reservations may be made by phone or online
- Dining reservations are recommended and may be made by calling 360-928-3211
- Rooms do not have Wi-Fi. Limited Wi-Fi access is available in the lobby only.

Lake Crescent Lodge
416 Lake Crescent Road
Port Angeles, WA 98363
888-896-3818 or 360-928-3211

Note that while Lake Crescent Lodge is located within Olympic National Park, you do not need an Olympic National Park pass to access or stay at the lodge.

Log Cabin Resort

Located on the shore of Lake Crescent, Log Cabin Resort offers an abundance of choices perfect for the National Park experience. Choose from Lakeside Chalets, Rustic Cabins, Camping Log Cabins, and Lodge Rooms, as well as full hook up RV and tent camping sites, all providing different levels of amenities, from rustic and sparse to comfortable and cozy. Be sure to ask for a lake or mountain view when making your reservation. Note that the resort is open from mid-May to early October.

Log Cabin Resort
3183 East Beach Road
Port Angeles, WA 98363
360-928-3325

Sol Duc Hot Springs Resort

Sol Duc Hot Spring Resort's rustic cabins are perfect as a home base for exploring Olympic National Park or simply soaking up the beauty of the Sol Duc Area...and the hot springs!

Amenities at the resort include large and small hot mineral-spring pools, massage therapists, a poolside deli, restaurant, gift shop, and convenience store.

>Sol Duc Hot Springs Resort
>12076 Sol Duc Hot Springs Road
>Port Angeles, WA 98363
>888-896-3818

- Open: March - October

Chito Beach Resort

Your exploration of the northwestern corner of the Olympic Peninsula is rewarded with a truly unique and special place to stay, the Chito Beach Resort. Occupying a small rocky point that extends out into the strait, this quaint resort welcomes guests with

six private cabins, each located at the water's edge and offering their own captivating views of the Strait of Juan de Fuca. Choose the "Cast Away" to enjoy a private sunset for two as you watch the sun slowly sink behind Shipwreck Point while waves toss against the rocks below, or perhaps select the "Bird House" and watch the dawn bring the new day from the east while you sit on your deck enjoying a warm cup of coffee. Four other cabins remain, including the most popular of which, the "Rock House". Here, guests can sit on a large deck and enjoy a commanding view stretching all the way from east to west, as well as across the entire strait to Canada. You'll want to sit for hours as you watch for orcas, gray whales, and humpbacks, as well as abundant wildlife close to shore, including sea lions, otters, bald eagles, and even perhaps a bobcat at the water's edge. And if you do spot a whale, then it's time to spring to action, as guests are encouraged to ring the "Whale Bell" so everyone can share in the excitement!

Return from a day of exploring the Olympic Peninsula and join your gracious hosts, Matt and Tamara, around the cozy fire pit to share your tales of the day's adventures and perhaps meet a new friend or two.

- Check-In Time: 3:00 p.m.
- Check-Out Time: 11:00 a.m.
- All cabins are non-smoking
- No guests under age 18 permitted
- No pets are allowed
- No boat or trailer parking is available
- Guests of the Rock House and Bird House will need to ascend steep ladders to reach their sleeping quarters, so please keep this in mind when making your reservations
- Ray's Grocery is located next door and offers gas and snacks, but little in the way of dinner or breakfast items

Note that due to septic system constraints, occupancy is limited to two people per cabin.

Chito Beach Resort
7639 Highway 112
Sekiu, WA 98381
360-963-2581
ChitoBeach@gmail.com

The Chito Beach Resort is located 7.5 miles west of Sekiu.

The Cabins at Beaver Creek

Located near the town of Sappho, The Cabins at Beaver Creek welcome guests after a day of exploration with a slower pace that beckons them to stroll through the farm, say "Hello" to a horse, goat or cow, explore an old moss-covered bridge slowly being reclaimed by a forest of maple trees, and then sit down around a campfire to enjoy some toasty S'mores before the night sky begins another stellar performance.

The owners, John and Michelle, have made sure each of the four cabins is well appointed with comfortable queen-sized beds and quality cotton linens, well equipped kitchens, fire places, large bathrooms with six foot tub/showers, hair dryers, coffee makers, private porches and more.

> The Cabins at Beaver Creek
> 272 Rixon Road
> Beaver, WA 98305
> 360-327-3867

Directions: Drive south on Hwy 113/Burnt Mountain Road after the junction with Hwy 112 and turn right at the junction with Hwy 101. Rixon Road is the first road on the right.

Note: If you are planning on eating before arriving at The Cabins at Beaver Creek, you may choose to eat at the Hungry Bear Café, located 2 miles east of Sappho on Hwy 101. They are open from 11:00 a.m. until 7:00 p.m. or 8:00 p.m., depending on how busy they are. 360-327-3225 (See page 147 for additional options.)

Historic Lake Quinault Lodge

Located on the shores of Lake Quinault, historic Lake Quinault Lodge greets guests with an ambiance found in the classic lodges of America's National Parks. Warm wood timbers, rustic furnishings, and a majestic wood-burning fireplace all invite you to sit for a spell, relax, and be taken back to 1926, the year in which the lodge was built. Then make your way outside to enjoy the patio, stroll across the large lawn, or walk down to the lake's edge to enjoy the view.

You'll also find the Lake Quinault Museum and General Store within walking distance, as well as a collection of lakeside trailheads nearby.

Lake Quinault Lodge
345 South Shore Road
Quinault, WA 98575
360-288-2900

www.Discover-Washington.com

REPLACE YOUR HOTELS WITH CAMPING IN A PACWESTY VAN?

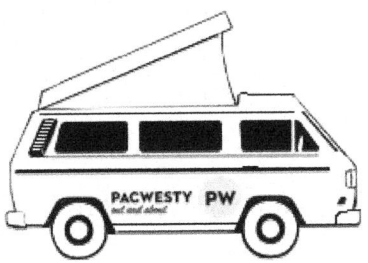

Want to add a bit of fun camping adventure to your exploration of the northern Olympic Peninsula? Then spend each night in a campervan instead of a hotel. The Olympic Peninsula offers an abundance of campgrounds and boondocking sites all along your journey.

We highly recommend the folks at PacWesty. Conveniently located on Bainbridge Island, PacWesty offers a fleet of fully equipped and expertly maintained VW Vanagons outfitted with everything you need, from camp chairs and towels to sleeping bags and cookware. In addition, they can help you rent all kinds of outdoor toys, including kayaks, paddleboards, bikes, and more. Best of all, Greg and his crew at PacWesty make it easy to rent. Just drop off your car, pick up your van and hit the road! Learn more at www.PacWesty.com

PacWesty
7869 NE Day Road W., Unit 206
Bainbridge Island, WA 98110
888-212-3546
Adventures@PacWesty.com

Phone Numbers Washington Road Trips - Northern Olympic Peninsula

- Adventures Through Kayaking: 360-417-3015
- Alexander's Castle: 360-344-4400
- Bishop Victorian Hotel: 833-254-2469
- Chito Beach Resort: 360-963-2581
- Discover Pass: 866-320-9933
- Fort Worden Lodging: 360-344-4434
- Hoh Rainforest Visitor Center: 360-374-6925
- Hungry Bear Café: 360-327-3225
- Hurricane Ridge Visitor Center: 360-565-3131
- Lake Crescent Lodge: 888-896-3818 or 360-928-3211
- Lake Quinault Lodge: 888-896-3818 or 360-288-2900
- Les Schwab Tire Center – Port Angeles – 360-452-7691
- Les Schwab Tire Center – Sequim – 360-683-7261
- Olympic National Park Visitor Center: 360-565-3130
- Puget Sound Express / Whale Watching: 360-385-5288
- Port Townsend WaterSports: 360-379-3608
- The Cabins at Beaver Creek – 360-327-3867
- The Palace Hotel: 360-385-0773
- Washington State Ferries: 888-808-7977 or 206-464-6400
- Washington State Parks Permit: 360-902-8844

Road Trip Washington's Olympic Peninsula

Washington's Olympic Peninsula has always been somewhat of a mystery, but now it's an adventurous and perfectly planned 6-day road trip! Set out to discover this exciting world that varies from high alpine peaks and lofty hiking trails to long sandy beaches and captivating ocean vistas. Stay at and explore the busy Victorian seaport of Port Townsend, visit a historic lighthouse, tour a vintage airplane museum, kayak on the Strait of Juan de Fuca, see majestic orcas, humpbacks, and gray whales, sleep in your very own castle, stand in the quietest place in the United States, explore unique shops, eat at great restaurants, meet friendly people, and so much more!

Your perfect Northern Olympic Peninsula road trip awaits...and it's already planned for you!

Available Now at Retailers Throughout Washington and Online

Now Enjoy An Oregon Coast Road Trip!

Oregon Road Trips – Oregon Coast Edition

Just as with this road trip, you'll explore the grandeur of Oregon's dramatic coastline during an adventurous 9-day road trip from Astoria south to Brookings. You'll journey along Oregon's beautiful Highway 101 as you discover countless scenic beaches, tour historic lighthouses, wander through quaint beach towns, watch whales spouting just off shore, ride in the cab of a 1925 steam locomotive, eat tasty Dungeness Crab fresh off the boat...or catch your own, stay in historic hotels, explore unique shops, meet friendly people and so much more. Best of all...everything is already planned for you!

Your perfect Oregon Coast road trip awaits!

Available Now at Retailers Throughout Oregon, Discover-Oregon.com and Online

What to See, Do & Explore on the Oregon Coast!

At 363 miles long, Oregon's scenic coastline is filled with countless natural wonders and attractions to see, do, and explore. Hike to a high bluff to watch for whales, walk a long sandy beach, explore a historic lighthouse, catch a live Dungeness crab, join in the fun of a sandcastle building contest, even ride aboard an old-fashioned steam train. The problem is...how do you uncover all of these activities to get the most out of your trip? The solution is *The Oregon Coast Guide*. Inside these pages, you'll discover over 200 fun and adventurous things to see, do and explore while visiting the Oregon Coast, complete with descriptions, photos, maps, tips, a whale watching guide and much more.

Available Now at Retailers Throughout Oregon, Discover-Oregon.com and Online

DISCOVER THE COLUMBIA RIVER GORGE!

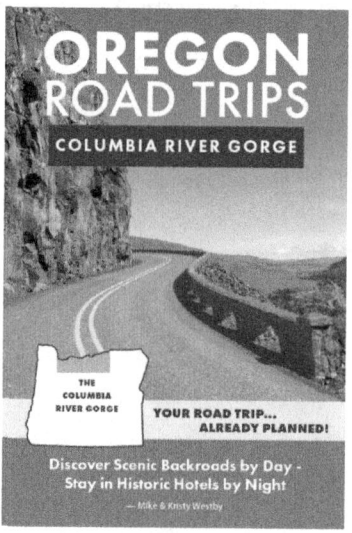

Oregon Road Trips – Columbia River Gorge Edition

Journey along the Oregon and Washington sides of the Columbia River Gorge as you spend five days discovering its majestic waterfalls, flying in a vintage 2-seater biplane, hiking through the historic Mosier Tunnels, stepping into the void on an exciting zip line tour, walking amidst the Gorge's beautiful spring wildflowers, finding your next favorite book at Oregon's oldest bookstore, and even spotting Giraffes, Zebras, Camels, Ostriches and more!

Your Columbia River Gorge road trip awaits, and it's already planned for you!

Available Now at Retailers Throughout Oregon, Discover-Oregon.com and Online

ROAD TRIP OREGON'S MAJESTIC MT. HOOD!

Oregon Road Trips – Mt. Hood Edition

An alpine Oregon Road Trip adventure is waiting for you!

Set out on an exciting Oregon road trip where every night ends at a charming historic hotel, finishing with majestic Timberline Lodge at 6,000' on the south shoulder of Mt. Hood! Explore the Historic Columbia River Highway, hike the unique Mosier Tunnels route, visit Oregon's oldest bookstore, walk among the Columbia River Gorge's colorful spring wildflowers, fly in a vintage 2-seater biplane, ride to over 7,000' on the Magic Mile Chairlift, discover the rustic and remote 1889 Cloud Cap Inn on Mt. Hood's eastern flank, and so much more.

Available Now at Retailers Throughout Oregon, Discover-Oregon.com and Online

DISCOVER A NORTHEAST OREGON ROAD TRIP!

Oregon Road Trips – Northeast Edition

Just as with this road trip guide, we've already laid out an exciting 9-day journey through Northeast Oregon's scenic backroads and byways for you. Along the way, you'll ride aboard a historic steam train, wander Oregon ghost towns, ascend in a cable tram to over 8,000', stay at the Wallowa Lake Lodge, board the Sumpter Valley Dredge, explore Cottonwood Canyon, ride the rails on a 2-seater, explore unique shops, eat at great restaurants, meet friendly people and so much more!

Your perfect Northeast Oregon road trip awaits, and it's already planned for you!

Available Now at Retailers Throughout Oregon, Discover-Oregon.com and Online

AND ANOTHER GREAT ROAD TRIP IS READY!

Oregon Road Trips – Southeast Edition

If you enjoyed exploring the Northern Olympic Peninsula, then you're sure to enjoy exploring remote Southeast Oregon. As with this title, you'll simply turn each page as you motor along and choose which points of interest to stop at and explore during your day's journey, *all while making your way toward that evening's lodging in a historic Oregon hotel.*

You'll drive to the top of 9,734' Steens Mountain, stay in the 1923 Frenchglen Hotel, explore the remote Leslie Gulch, see how stage coaches are built, dig for fossils, hike "Crack in the Ground", look for wild Mustangs, eat at a truly unique and remote Oregon restaurant, marvel at the geologic wonders of the Journey Through Time Scenic Byway and so much more!

Available Now at Retailers Throughout Oregon, Discover-Oregon.com and Online

SOUTHWEST OREGON AWAITS!

Oregon Road Trips – Southwest Edition

Visit 13 historic covered bridges, spend a night in Crater Lake Lodge, discover a vintage aircraft museum, enjoy a play in Ashland, explore deep into the Oregon Caves, wander an Oregon ghost town, see some of Oregon's most beautiful waterfalls, tour the Applegate Wine Trail, and so much more on your 9-day road trip through Southwest Oregon. As with our other Oregon Road Trip books, you'll simply motor along while you discover Oregon, and finish each night at a unique historic hotel!

Your perfect Southwest Oregon road trip awaits, and it's already planned for you!

Available Now at Retailers Throughout Oregon, Discover-Oregon.com and Online

DISCOVER THE COLUMBIA RIVER GORGE

Cutting a deep gorge between Oregon and Washington, the majestic Columbia River Gorge is filled with scenic vistas, graceful waterfalls, amazing attractions, captivating history, and countless adventures, and they are all waiting for you in the *Columbia River Gorge - An Explorer's Guide*. With this guide you'll discover the many waterfalls of "Waterfall Alley", walk among the gorge's colorful spring wildflowers, fly in a vintage 2-seater biplane over Mt. Hood, see over 300 restored antique motorcars and aeroplanes up close, explore the Hood River "Fruit Loop", hike classic gorge trails, visit Oregon's oldest bookstore, discover some great new cycling roads and routes, watch world-class sailboarding, see giraffes, zebras, camels, and bison, stay a night or two or three at one of the gorge's historic hotels, watch a master glass blower create a stunning trout out of glass, eat the biggest ice cream cone in your life, and so much more!

Available Now at Retailers Throughout Oregon, Discover-Oregon.com and Online

DISCOVER CENTRAL OREGON

Central Oregon is a big place. To the west, high Cascade lakes and snowy peaks offer a world of alpine adventure, while to the east, the high desert beckons travelers to another world, one filled with thrilling experiences and geological wonders. In between is a land of scenic vistas, majestic waterfalls, amazing attractions, and countless outdoor and indoor adventures just waiting to be explored, and they're all here for you in the new *Central Oregon - An Explorer's Guide!* Use this guide to discover over 150 unique attractions, destinations, and experiences where you'll discover nine thundering waterfalls, set out on a moonlight kayaking adventure, walk among WWII era aircraft, hike through Oregon's high desert, ride a summer chairlift up Mt. Bachelor to enjoy some amazing alpine views, drive to the top of Paulina Peak, watch world-class rock climbing up close, paddleboard and kayak on the slow flowing Deschutes River, explore an ancient lava tube, and much more!

Available Now at Retailers Throughout Oregon, Discover-Oregon.com and Online

WE RECOMMEND...

Les Schwab Tire Centers

If you're on the road and have a flat tire, brake issues or a similar problem, we highly recommend the very helpful folks at your nearby Les Schwab Tire Center. You'll find locations in Sequim and Port Angeles. Their phone numbers are listed on page 162.

Hama Hama Oysters

It's not the Olympic Peninsula without seafood, and it's not seafood without oysters, and it's not oysters without Hama Hama!

If you're driving north along Hwy 101 to the Northern Olympic Peninsula, then be sure to stop in at Hama Hama to enjoy fresh local oysters, clams, and crabs, as well as house-smoked oysters and salmon, live and cooked crab, fresh salmon, and locally produced ice cream, cheeses, grass-fed beef, chocolate, and other treats. You can also mail order anytime of the year!

> 35846 N. US Hwy 101
> Lilliwaup, WA 98555
> 360-877-5811
> www.HamaHamaOysters.com

75 Classic Rides: Oregon

From an after-work ride through Portland's neighborhood streets or a family cycle along the flat Willamette Valley Scenic Bikeway, to a multi-day tour in the salty breezes of the Oregon coast—if you're seeking the best bike trails in Oregon, you'll find plenty of blacktop bliss in Jim Moore's *75 Classic Rides: Oregon*.

Olympic Mountain Ice Cream

Made with the finest ingredients grown locally in the Pacific Northwest, Olympic Mountain Ice Cream offers a delectable collection of handcrafted artisan ice creams, gelatos, and sorbets. Look for them in small markets while traveling the Olympic Peninsula.

Are You a Disneyland Fan?

Enjoy a fascinating and entertaining book which reveals over 250 of the fun hidden secrets and story elements that the Disney Imagineers have purposely hidden for Disneyland guests to find and enjoy, complete with 225 photos!

Available online, as well as at the prestigious Walt Disney Family Museum, the Walt Disney Boyhood Home, and the Walt Disney Hometown Museum.

Want Even More Disneyland Secrets?

Discover the in-depth stories behind 50 magical story elements of Disneyland, *many of which are published here for the very first time.* Compiled from extensive research and lengthy interviews with Disney Legends, Imagineers, and other Disney notables.

Available online and at the prestigious Walt Disney Family Museum, the Walt Disney Boyhood Home, and the Walt Disney Hometown Museum.

Are You a Walt Disney World Fan?

See and experience Walt Disney World in an entirely new way! Written by Oregon author Mike Fox, *The Hidden Secrets & Stories of Walt Disney World* reveals over 500 of the fun secret story elements that the Disney Imagineers have hidden throughout all four parks, complete with more than 400 photos.

Available online, as well as at the Walt Disney Hometown Museum and the Walt Disney Boyhood Home.

Camp Attitude

"Changing lives one camper at a time!"

Camp Attitude provides a welcoming camp experience for disabled youth and their families. Here, children with special needs can participate in all of the fun, games, excitement and interaction of a thrilling week-long "summer camp" experience, all for a nominal fee, thanks to donations from contributors who enjoy seeing a smile on a child's face...and a squirt gun in their hand!

Camp Attitude is a faith-based non-profit organization, and donations may be made by visiting their web site at www.CampAttitude.org

>Camp Attitude
>PO Box 2017
>45829 S Santiam Hwy
>Foster, OR 97345
>541-401-1052

Notes

Made in the USA
Middletown, DE
21 June 2022